Shuddha

Rachna Chhachhi, PhD, Holistic Nutrition, is a certified nutritional therapist and holistic cancer coach. She is World Health Organization (WHO) certified in malnutrition and a certified yoga and Ayurveda teacher. She has her own practice for holistic treatment for cancer and lifestyle diseases across 27 countries under *RachnaRestores*, and her own internationally accredited holistic health coach certification programme. She has 200+ coaches globally certified by her who are practising holistic healing and helping patients achieve better quality of life.

Rachna also heads the Asia wing of *The Center for Advancement in Cancer Education | BeatCancer.Org*, a non-profit global organization headquartered in Pennsylvania, USA, whose mission is to help people beat cancer via nutrition, lifestyle and other immune-boosting therapies. She has been a health writer for 20 years and has published health columns with *BW Businessworld*, *Business Today*, *Outlook Business* and *Times of India (TOI Blogs)*.

Rachna has treated patients for chronic diseases like metastatic and secondary cancers, rheumatoid arthritis, psoriasis, lupus, multiple sclerosis, scleroderma, fibromyalgia and other autoimmune conditions; lifestyle diseases like type two diabetes, hypertension, high cholesterol, heart blockages, obesity; and hormonal issues like polycystic ovary syndrome (PCOS), hypothyroidism, etc. She is regularly invited to renowned international conferences as a keynote speaker to share her case studies on disease reversal without medication, via integrative healing therapies.

Shuddha is her fourth book.

Shuddha

Your Journey Within to
Stay Cleansed

RACHNA CHHACHHI

Published by
Rupa Publications India Pvt. Ltd 2022
7/16, Ansari Road, Daryaganj
New Delhi 110002

Sales centres:
Allahabad Bengaluru Chennai
Hyderabad Jaipur Kathmandu
Kolkata Mumbai

Copyright © Rachna Chhachhi 2022

The views and opinions expressed in this book
are the author's own and the facts are as reported by her
which have been verified to the extent possible,
and the publishers are not in any way liable for the same.

All rights reserved.

No part of this publication may be reproduced, transmitted,
or stored in a retrieval system, in any form or by any means,
electronic, mechanical, photocopying, recording or otherwise,
without the prior permission of the publisher.

ISBN: 978-93-5520-190-4

First impression 2022

10 9 8 7 6 5 4 3 2 1

The moral right of the author has been asserted.

Printed at Saurabh Printers Pvt. Ltd, Noida

This book is sold subject to the condition that it shall not,
by way of trade or otherwise, be lent, resold, hired out, or otherwise circulated,
without the publisher's prior consent, in any form of binding or cover other than
that in which it is published.

Contents

Foreword by Dr Hansaji Yogendra — *vii*

Chapter Zero: *Walk This Path with Me* — *xi*

Part 1: Understanding Toxins

Chapter 1: They're Around Us and Inside Us	3
Chapter 2: 21 Signs Your Body Has a Toxin Build-Up	19
Chapter 3: Why My Shuddha Programme Works	27
Chapter 4: Preparing for a Holistically Shuddha Life	33

Part 2: Implementing the Four Phases

Chapter 1: Repair the Gut—the First Seven Days	55
Chapter 2: Release the Toxins in Three Weeks	65
Chapter 3: Reactivate your Rhythm—Four Weeks	74
Chapter 4: Restore Your Balance	86
Chapter 5: Understanding Your Foods	93
Chapter 6: Eating Shuddha Recipes	98

Part 3: Emotional Detox

Chapter 1: Toxins and Stress	151
Chapter 2: Toxins and Well-Being	155
Chapter 3: Emotional Shuddhi	163

Part 4: The Holistic Detox Balance

Chapter 1: Physical and Emotional Detox   169
Chapter 2: Attitude Is Everything   172

Part 5: The Shuddha Life

Chapter 1: 11 Signs That You Have Been Detoxed   179
Chapter 2: How to Live the Detox Life—Travel Tips   185
Chapter 3: How to Live the Detox Life—Eating Out   190

References   193

Foreword

Purity is a very important concept in yoga. It is the first *niyama*, known as *shaucha*, and the yogi is expected to be clean in thought, word and deed. Spiritual progress cannot take place without releasing impurity, and we tend to gather impurities both at the physical and emotional level. Physical impurities are, of course, the result of poor food habits and environmental pollution, and it is our thoughts, stress, the information we consume from media, difficult relationships, etc., that muddy our mind. Well, regardless of whether one is a spiritual aspirant or not, the need to keep one's body and mind pure, even if to only stay in good health, is a must.

Rachna's book comes at a time when Mother Nature has rapped us hard on the knuckles for being impure and for making the environment impure. It's been more than two years now and we are still reeling under the impurities we have heaped on ourselves and the planet. *Shuddha*, besides shattering the myths that surround detoxification, or purification, if you prefer to call it that, also speaks about how simple it actually is to lead a life that is toxin-free and, as a result, a healthier and high-immunity lifestyle. Rachna has delved into Ayurveda and yoga, and incorporated the best practices of both these ancient and traditional Indian systems Rachna Chhachhi has been a promising student of The Yoga Institute. I wish her lots of luck, and I'm sure her book will be a resounding success.

Dr Hansaji Yogendra
President, The Yoga Institute

The Yoga Institute (TYI), Mumbai, India, was founded in 1918 by Shri Yogendraji, and is the oldest yoga centre in the world. It has branches across the world including Hong Kong, Costa Rica, Uruguay, France and Thailand. TYI received the prestigious Prime Minister's Award for Outstanding Contribution for Promotion and Development of Yoga for the year 2018–19. The 200-Hour Teacher Training Course (TTC) conforms to the Yoga Certification Board (YCB), the Ministry of AYUSH and the Yoga Alliance, USA.

Chapter Zero

Walk This Path with Me

I am a student for life. When it comes to healing and healing energies, I need to nourish my mind with new knowledge at least once a year. Since 2008, I have re-educated myself in the area of holistic nutrition and disease reversal—one aspect at a time. And this is the reason I believe I remain healed from what doctors call an incurable condition—rheumatoid arthritis (RA).

We are all holistic beings and the Universe has put little remedies in every corner of the world. Learning each one of them step by step helps me incorporate some of these learnings to get better patient outcomes. Today, I am thankful that I get clinically evidenced outcomes and it is because I combine the power of holistic nutrition, nutritional science with Ayurveda, yoga, pranayama and meditation. It is only now that the clinical studies on the healing effects of Ayurveda, yoga, pranayama and meditation—clubbed as mind-body interventions—have been published, showcasing the strength with which they repair the mind and body. Hence, my practice is evidence informed, some of which are quoted in this book as well, in the section pertaining to clinical references.

In 2008, after I healed myself by ditching methotrexate[1] and immunosuppressants with only the power of holistic nutrition, I began my journey of becoming a healer and a student. To heal others, it was my duty to educate myself to the best of my ability, coupled with pure intentions in helping them. In my previous life (my life is divided into two births: pre RA and post RA), I was in the corporate sector, heading business development for a large multinational company. The discovery of this new healing path made me excited and nervous all at once. There was the exhilaration of defeating my diagnosis and prognosis clinically and there was the mammoth task of walking the path to help others like me who had nowhere to go. So I set simple goals for myself: I first re-educated myself in what the world calls alternative treatments, but what we all know have the ability to repair the human mind and body beyond comprehension.

The first stop was to complete a certification in nutritional therapy in order to obtain a powerful understanding of how plants in every form—food or supplements—can heal us. This triggered a long journey of establishing my nutrition practice online and treating patients globally. I have worked online since 2009, when the rest of the world was working offline.

I had learnt yoga during my own healing process and I added tenets from this to help patients get better. As my practice grew, the need for mothers to understand how to take care of their infants kept coming to me. So I amassed knowledge in infant and child nutrition via a WHO-certified course. My uphill, but beautiful, journey started attracting cancer patients suffering from side effects of chemotherapy, radiation, immunotherapy, hormone therapy and wasting from the cancer itself. While I treated them successfully with nutritional therapy, it was important to delve deep into how cancer ravages our body and how we can repair it. So my next quest for learning, as a student, was to become a certified cancer nutrition expert from *Beat Cancer*, a non-profit cancer institute founded by Susan Silberstein, who lost her husband to cancer in 1977. Susan's zeal and the knowledge, captured in that course, helped me get clinically successful outcomes for various late-stage cancer patients.

However, the cancer cases were not just growing but there was cancer recurrence—metastasis is a huge cancer problem today. Understanding metastasis is very difficult and so I reached out to the best in medical care—Johns Hopkins—to get certified in cancer metastasis.

During one of my quests for knowledge, I signed up for the 200-hour yoga teacher training certification course at The Yoga Institute. It was a turning point in my life. It's not like I had not practised yoga before. I had been taught by an able teacher and since 2007, I had practised yoga to heal my deformed joints and get mobility. But this, somehow, felt different.

Entering the serene environment of the institute, interacting with Hansaji, whose innate wisdom, calmness and knowledge seeped into me like a dry sponge absorbs water; I felt refreshed and grateful all at once. I learnt about the connection between yoga, Ayurveda and inner peace. So when I started penning down this book, there was no better person to endorse this healing path than Hansaji herself. I am so grateful to her for agreeing to write the Foreword.

My practice and clinical outcomes became even better after this experience. Yogic living can help re-establish the homeostatic balance by releasing toxins and making physical and emotional balance aligned, thereby enhancing quality of life. This balance pushes disease out as a natural consequence of the yogic life.

After so many years of healing thousands of patients across the world, there is one simple truth I have witnessed, which we all tend to miss—at the deep end of what works to heal ourselves is to stay detoxed. Healing always, *always*, begins with the purity of the mind and body. Whenever we are imbalanced, we attract disease. When the earth became imbalanced, we faced the pandemic. Hence, integrating the balance again means releasing and shedding the toxins and making space for nutrients, healing energies and blessings. That's why, the first step towards healing yourself is to detox continuously and make yourself shuddha—mind, body and soul.

The keyword is continuous.

The detoxification process is a complex one. Often misunderstood as colon cleansing or fasting, true detoxification contains healing foods, calming breath work and a lifestyle that can help the liver release toxins faster every day. This enables reduced oxidative stress, bloating, reduction in fatty liver and increases brain agility and aids weight balance.

Don't fall for quick fixes, shortcuts, fad diets or miracle cures because they do not exist. The only miracle that exists is within you—it is the power to heal yourself. That does not mean that you will not enjoy yourself or indulge in flavoursome pleasures. Don't become boring! Ask anyone who knows me, I am not boring—I have my indulgences. The key is in the balance. Detox yourself on a daily basis so that when you indulge, the body naturally rejects any indulgences and they stop affecting you. After a while of continuous practise, you reach a point where you can indulge guilt-free because you know that you have made your body so strong and shuddha that it will not tolerate any toxins to stay inside for long.

For many of you, this may sound difficult or obscure but it is quite easy to do. In *Shuddha*, I have made it even easier, giving very specific steps for you to follow and reach your goal of being disease-free and emotionally and physically balanced. Everything I have written in this book has been clinically tried and tested and evidenced via symptomatic relief, scans and blood reports showing improvement as well as a noticeable increase in quality of life. There is a step-by-step process to cleanse ourselves and incorporate practices as our 'new normal'. All these steps are written in this book. There are 50+ delightful recipes—what more could you want? The focus here is to live a long and healthy life and remain shuddha, and yet not be a tiresome health freak who judges and lectures others.

Before you dismiss following a healthier lifestyle because you don't have time, read this: I always found time to nourish my mind despite everybody saying that I am too busy or lamenting that they themselves are too busy to pause and smell the roses. So my understanding of your lack of time to nurture yourself is that you have not made yourself a priority. Today, as you read this book, make *you* important to you.

In Ayurveda, I have not referred to the *doshas*, that information is already in the public domain. I move a step ahead—when we have the doshas, we have to look at how to move ahead and heal ourselves from them via a mind-body balance. Hence, this book combines the self-healing principles of Ayurveda with clinically evidenced nutritional healing to help you experience the path of being shuddha via self-nurturing. When you nurture yourself, your toxins disappear, leaving you cleansed and *swastha*, to welcome the joys of life and good health.

Let's welcome the joy of living with purity.

You make space for nutrients by the release of toxins.

PART ONE

Understanding Toxins

I inhaled the air around me. And then I fell sick.

Chapter 1

They're Around Us and Inside Us

When I began writing this book, I did not know where to start. This is my fourth book but the subject is more complex than we all view it as. We are not living in the deep jungles, mountains or clean beaches. We all live in the overwhelming hustle of city life and work on a daily basis. Due to the lack of time in a fast-paced life, people reach out to cleanse themselves in whatever way they are taught to. So the presence of detoxification programmes attracts them like a magnet and the miraculous results of those who have followed it temporarily attract and mesmerize each one of us. The frustrations of our daily life and the fatigue vanish temporarily with the hope of a fairy-tale ending after doing a seven-day detox.

The rising cases of skin allergies, asthma, bronchitis, kidney damage, gut issues, bloating, PCOS, constipation, chronic fatigue, depression, acne, eczema, inflammation and headaches are everywhere around us. Young children under the age of five are also suffering from such issues. And the biggest cause for this is a single word– toxins.

What I have listed above are just the diagnosed ramifications of toxins. The emotional ramifications of these deadly anti-nutrients inside our bloodstream, digestive system and organs cause severe anxiety, nausea, mood swings and pessimism. Despite all this, when we inhale the air, go for a walk on the concrete road, eat the healthy vegetarian but refined food, we never link anything back to our physical and emotional toxins. Many studies have shown that maternal exposure to the common and ever-present forms of industrial pollution hanging in the air we breathe can harm the immune system of a little baby.[1] To realize that this negative impact of toxins is passed along to successive generations, weakening the body's defences against infections such as the influenza virus, should in itself be a wake-up call to each one of us concerned about the current pandemic.

The irony is that toxins are not just from the environment and pollution. Even if we are sitting indoors, protecting ourselves from the pandemic or polluted air, we are still inhaling and building toxins every minute in the form of plastic in our water, dust, toxins from products we use and emotional distress. When these toxins build up inside our bloodstream, mind or colon, they lead to an internal bodily environment of welcoming diseases. Carcinogens from non-stick pans or the emotional toxicity of a bad relationship are all toxins that need to be removed on a continuous basis for you to feel energized, cleansed and stay disease-free.

A build-up of toxins in your body suppresses your immune system. And with the pandemic that we have been witnessing in the last couple of years, the most important health goal that everybody needs to have is a strong immune system to ride over COVID-19 and the side effects to be able to live a long and healthy life.

In medical terms, a toxin is defined as
any kind of poison that spoils our health.

A true detoxification programme then should not only focus on consuming green smoothies or turmeric lattes. Detoxification also needs to happen via our skin, gut and mind. Stripping of the electromagnetic waves around us, the repetitive stress our body and organs go through, the build-up of excess sugar, bad fat and stress due to lack of sleep and a poor lifestyle are all factors to consider for living a detoxed life. A complete detoxification from everything that is harming us has to be done on a daily basis in order to achieve an energetic and wonderful quality of life. Why? Because these toxins are around us every minute of our day and going for a stopgap arrangement of a short detoxification programme and then coming back to inhale or absorb these toxins again makes no sense. We bathe daily, we go to the bathroom every day and if we do not, even something as small as constipation can build up severe toxins in the body and cause pain and discomfort. So imagine living with toxins for months and years on end and feeling unwell, and not knowing that this is because of the toxic load you are carrying every day.

THE PROBLEM WITH DETOXIFICATION PROGRAMMES

Most detox diets are exactly that—diets. A diet is not sustainable. It cannot be incorporated into your lifestyle. For example, without sweating a few times a week, the detoxification process is not complete for our skin; otherwise the gut gets overwhelmed. A sudden onslaught of high fibre from green smoothies can leave you nauseous and feeling ill for most of the time that you are on a detox.

Too much water can hurt you too. Most detox diets talk about drinking copious amounts of water which can put pressure on your kidneys. Not only that, excess water in the body starts diluting nutrients and these nutrients are not able to reach the body parts that they need to reach for nourishing them. The result? A bloated you with poor kidney function and no energy because of low nutrient absorption. Not to forget the frequent rounds of going to the bathroom in the middle of the night, hence interrupting your sound sleep. Without sound sleep, the body cannot repair itself.

It's not like we are not aware that we need a detoxification programme. This is evident from the number of books and programmes on detoxification, cleansing and short-term diets that claim to clean out your gut and release the toxins. Every single stopgap diet programme you do, every seven-day cleanse programme that you go on, is not long-lasting and is unsustainable to carry on in everyday life. Not only that, continuing a detox programme for a longer period of time can cause muscle wasting, sensitive gut and chronic fatigue. So what you set out to do as healthy can cause problems because it is a temporary solution and not a permanent one.

While the claims are true and some of them do deliver, I have a basic issue with short-term diet programmes in the first place. If the toxins around us are omnipresent and we have to achieve good health, how can we rely on a short-term programme that will clean out everything from the past but not control anything in the present or the future? This means that every three months or six months, as per what we choose, we get into shocking our immune system, digestive system and body to cause the release of something that is harmful for us. But in implementing this, the shock that we give to our immune system can itself derail our immune system's response. Our mind and body, which the immune system controls, needs gentle nurturing and daily self-care. In the next few pages of this book, you will understand how to implement self-love and self-care to be able to release your toxins and get the highest energy levels and the best glowing skin you deserve, without upsetting your immune system and negotiating extremes. Our goal is to be gentle, nurturing and loving towards ourselves so that we can detox for the purpose of healing.

For a moment, let us look at the real meaning of detox as per Oxford dictionary:

Detox
noun
/ˈdiːtɒks/
1. a process or period of time in which one abstains from or rids the body of toxic or unhealthy substances; detoxification.

verb
/diːˈtɒks/
1. abstain from or rid the body of toxic or unhealthy substances.

Abstaining or getting rid of toxic substances is a daily process. Remember: you excrete stool daily and you need to. You urinate daily and you need to. You also eat daily and you need to do that to nourish yourself. So then, when there is a *daily* absorption of toxins in your skin, through the air you breathe, through the food you eat, why should you wait for three or six months to expel them? Why should you provide a home to these viruses, pathogens, chemicals, preservatives, cancer-causing substances? Especially if the home is your own body! Just like you have a daily cleansing routine of washing your face and body by having a bath every day, internal cleansing also needs to happen on a daily basis.

And that is why the entire logic of doing a one-week detox every few months is self-defeating. Of course there are benefits of that detox programme—you will reduce the load of the detox on your liver so the liver will function properly. You will feel fresher because you would have knocked off a few kilos. You would reduce your inflammation levels because you would be ingesting antioxidants in the form of plant-based foods and smoothies. *Temporarily*. Then, you will go back to your normal life and inflammation levels will start increasing again. Short changing yourself by thinking that you will party for three months and then again go for a detox may signal a yo-yo dieting message to your body and push it towards a fight-or-flight response.

> *Our immune system and our body*
> *respond to consistency.*

Weight cycling or the constant losing and gaining of weight (usually from diets), leads to adverse health consequences. In the absence of consistent healthy habits, yo-yo dieting (weight cycling) to lose weight by extreme detoxification and then getting back to a 'normal' life that had, in the first place, led to an increase in weight, puts pressure on the heart and can cause chronic fatigue, high risk of heart attack and even sudden death.

By most estimates, almost 80 per cent of the people who lose weight through a diet gradually regain it and end up being the same weight or even heavier than they were before they went on the diet. This is because once an individual loses weight, the body typically reduces the amount of energy expended at rest, during exercise and daily activities while increasing hunger. This combination of lower energy expenditure and hunger creates a 'perfect metabolic storm' of conditions for weight gain. As per a study published in the Endocrine Society's *Journal of Clinical Endocrinology and Metabolism*, this study shows that weight cycling can heighten a person's risk of death.[2]

And yet, the concept of detox to lose weight has been turned, twisted and bent out of shape, making it seem unattainable for many people who cannot fast, have health issues, are suffering from type two diabetes and therefore cannot stay hungry for extended periods of time or people with compromised immune systems and women with hormonal issues. It has also been converted to become a fad followed by people who want quick and easy results.

Fortunately, detoxification is a much simpler process and can be continued on a regular basis without feeling too much discomfort and staying on top of your health. And the results are often incredible—glowing skin, healthy hair and yes, weight loss!

So what are the toxins that you need to get rid of in order to start your own healing journey?

There are some toxins that we never take into account. Toxins are of three kinds:
1. Environmental
2. Edible
3. Emotional

ENVIRONMENTAL TOXINS

1. **Toxins through our skin.** We may purchase the most expensive toxin-free products for our skin, but the water we bathe in either has toxins or chemicals to treat those toxins. Very few of us have the luxury of bathing in pure

water without toxins. Our skin is our largest organ and it absorbs these toxins. In fact, a new research has unearthed links between poor male fertility and pollutants in water.[3]

2. **The waves around us.** You can't see them but your Wi-Fi, the mobile towers around you and the electromagnetic frequencies are causing fluctuations inside you. These are as toxic as the chemicals and artificial colours you ingest. Dr Beatrice Golomb, MD, PhD, professor of medicine at School of Medicine, University of California San Diego, says that publicly reported symptoms and experiences of a 'mystery illness' afflicting American and Canadian diplomats in Cuba and China strongly match known effects of pulsed radiofrequency (RF)/microwave electromagnetic (MW) radiation.[4] Sleep problems, headaches and cognitive issues were just some of the symptoms experienced with RF/MW radiation. The limitless stream of prompts and notifications from the Internet decreases our capacity for maintaining concentration on a single task. In a world where we are pushing for mindfulness to cure various kinds of diseases because mindfulness is clinically shown to reduce inflammation levels, the interference of anything with our body and mind that hinders its health becomes a toxin.

3. **Pollution.** This is an obvious one but with severe ramifications. We don't realize that the pollution from vehicles and industries is not just outside our homes, but also inside. Researchers have linked some environmental pollutants with diseases, a decreased lifespan and signs of premature aging, such as wrinkles and age spots.[5] In Italy, air pollution has also been linked to higher mortality in COVID-19 cases.[6] And the link between pollution and our liver has been well established for a long time.

4. **Lack of oxygen.** Lack of oxygen is rampant today because the polluted air we are breathing does not get cleansed by the presence of higher oxygen levels in the atmosphere. This is because we do not have enough greenery around us. This lack of oxygen helps damaged cells to grow and leads to an increased risk of cancer. In cancer patients, I have seen oxygen therapy work wonders to stabilize patients. But we never see lack of oxygen as a toxin because we are only looking at toxins from a perspective of *presence* of something harmful and not *absence* of something important. Higher levels of oxygen accelerate the detoxification process and make it natural and smooth, leading to a cleaner gut.

EDIBLE TOXINS

1. **Chemicals.** Pollutants such as lead, arsenic and pesticides cause non-alcoholic liver disease.[7] These are present everywhere—in the water we drink, the water we bathe in and the food we eat. When we go on a heavy plant-based diet, they often get absorbed by the plants from the soil they are present in.
2. **Bad fats.** Biting into a samosa once in a while or some pure ghee halwa is not a problem at all. But when we continuously eat fried items or saturated fats, the toxins start to build up. Bad fats can be an excess of saturated fats, fats present in deep-fried foods, which have the presence of aldehydes, and can increase the risk of neurodegenerative diseases and also certain types of cancers.[8] The particularly toxic kind of fats are the ones which are refried for the purpose of frying, very common in restaurant foods, even if you order in from the best

of restaurants or hotels. Sunflower oil and soybean oil when heated to high temperatures can be extremely toxic. Apart from these, the presence of saturated fats in our bloodstream has been shown to freeze and damage our cell membranes, leading to deposits in the entire body.[9] These saturated fats then lead to so many health issues—apart from weight gain, this can lead to a fatty liver, high cholesterol, high triglycerides, plaque-like deposits in the heart and the brain, increasing the risk of heart blockages and diseases like Alzheimer's, anxiety, depression, memory loss and dementia.[10] Bad fat roaming around in our body is a deadly toxin and needs to be expelled in order to reduce the risk of these diseases.

3. **Sugar.** It exists in many forms. If you stand up and say that you have given up all sweets and desserts and are still experiencing symptoms of a poor quality of life and high toxin load—check your carbohydrate content. Higher than 50 per cent intake of carbohydrates in your daily meal increases the sugar content in your body, increasing genetic risk of type two diabetes, heart disease and certain types of cancers.

4. **Imbalance.** An imbalance in the way we eat causes toxins to build up. Excessive carbohydrates, excessive protein, not enough natural fibre or vegetables or unsaturated fat, not enough exercise or over exercising are some of the imbalances that stop the toxins from being expelled. A large part of healthy and clean living arises from this balance. And it is this balance that is going to be explained further in the book.

EMOTIONAL TOXINS

1. **Lack of sleep.** We often compromise on sleep due to work and stress or toss and turn in the middle of the night because of severe anxiety. I have treated so many women with hormonal fluctuations, and a clear sign of this is chronic insomnia. They sleep for a couple of hours and then wake up at night, not being able to go back to sleep. Lack of sleep is probably the biggest toxic habit human beings have. Without seven to eight hours sleep on a daily basis, repair and rejuvenation does not take place. This makes our brain agitated, leading to the production of an acidic environment in our digestive system. This cycle of poor sleep leading to poor digestion makes our absorption of nutrients from food low. It also increases cravings and people who have less sleep crave high carbohydrates and sugary foods, which attract toxins to stay longer in the body. Funguses, like candida, feed on sugar to stay alive in the body. In the absence of sugar and high carbohydrates, funguses start dying out. However, with lack of sleep, the hunger hormones crave carbohydrates and hence it is a vicious cycle of attracting fungal infections. Lack of sleep also raises sugar levels in the body, increasing our risk of type two diabetes. And we all know that sugar is the biggest toxin in our bloodstream.
2. **Our response to stress.** The stress we accumulate is as much a toxin as the environmental toxins we are inhaling and absorbing through our skin. Combined with these toxins, stress can inhibit absorption of nutrients in our gut, weakening it. When our digestive system becomes weak and does not absorb nutrients from food, our immune system cannot stay strong. We experience stress

on an everyday basis and even when we are eating right, stress continues to release acids in the stomach. These acids deplete the digestive system and halt the healing process. Remember feeling gassy, bloated, acidic? That is your ferocious cycle of stress overproducing acids. This blocks absorption of nutrients. So without first helping repair your gut to start absorbing nutrients, putting pressure on your gut with an extreme detox programme can be really unhealthy. Ultimately, lowering absorption of nutrients leads to a poor immune response. This poor immune response definitely opens up an entire Pandora's box of infections and diseases.

Now that we have understood that high load of toxins leads to a poor immune system, let us look at the kind of diseases that are connected to the immune system.

1. Asthma
2. Bronchitis
3. Eczema
4. Autoimmune conditions—which medical science doesn't have a cure for yet
5. Depression
6. Risk for inflammation—which is the root cause of all lifestyle diseases
7. Risk of hormonal fluctuations—the number of cases of PCOS, hypothyroidism, obesity, hormonal acne or thinning scalp hair in young girls and women is increasing at an alarming rate
8. Increased risk of cancer

Hence, pretty much every disease you find fearful is linked to physical and emotional toxins in your body and mind.

A large part of toxin removal comes from understanding what they cause.

What is the biggest toxin around us? Plastic. We all know plastic is bad. Yet, what is our first choice of a feeding bottle for an infant? A plastic bottle. Polycarbonate baby bottles release bisphenol A (BPA).[11] BPA is one of the many man-made chemicals classified as endocrine disruptors, which alter the function of the endocrine system by mimicking the role of the body's natural hormones. Hormones are secreted through endocrine glands and serve different functions throughout the body.

I work with a lot of young girls and I would like to share the life journey of this beautiful young girl, Meghana, who I have known since she was a child. She was born premature and her immune system was underdeveloped. She did not have enough strength to suckle her mother's breast within the first seven to 10 days and, hence, the neonatal ward where she was admitted had to give her bottle milk and formula in order to keep her alive. As she regained her strength and stabilized, the parents of this little girl were delighted to take her home and she finally had the strength to suckle on her mother's milk, which was the nectar of life for her immune system. She was breastfed for seven months because her mother was very conscious of the fact that it was breast milk that would increase this preterm baby's immunity. However, the bottle feeding continued nightly, on the paediatrician's advice, as she was underweight. As she grew up, her sensitivity towards the environment was high. If it was too dry she would get a dry cough. If the place was polluted, she would get an asthma attack. This continued till she reached the age of 10 when she got nutrition and homeopathy treatments and her health began improving.

Simultaneously, something else was also happening—pre-puberty, this girl developed a lot of hair—facial hair, armpit hair and a lot more hair growth on her limbs compared to other girls in her age group. This made her feel embarrassed and underconfident. Finally, when she hit puberty at the age of 13, her journey of painful periods began. As she grew older, her clear skin started developing acne and the best efforts at eating the most nutritious foods, including fruits and vegetables could not make the acne go away. Her IgG and IgA levels (immunoglobulins) were high, which are immune response markers. And it was evident from her demeanour that her emotional sensitivity was much higher than young people her age. Finally, at the age of 18, she was clinically diagnosed with PCOS. She made repeated attempts through different nutrition programmes available to her, some highly recommended by various experts, but the acne refused to disappear and the painful periods did not stop.

Then Meghana discovered yoga. Combined with eating healthy, she started enjoying yoga and started releasing the anxiety around wanting flawless skin and less facial hair. She became so immersed in her yoga practice that she would let go of the world's worries every time she was with herself and her yoga music. And then, suddenly, her skin started to clear out. Her period pain started to reduce and began to get regular, almost arriving on the dot. Today, this young woman is 24 years old and her quality of life is drastically restored because she chose to not look at the toxins inside her body since birth as unidimensional.

From day one, the BPA from the plastic bottles was leaching onto her underdeveloped immune system and as a preterm baby, while the formula milk was saving her life, the plastic pieces were becoming the endocrine disruptors which would play out much later in her life. Getting those plastic disruptors out of her body was not possible with the short-term programmes of detox diets, eating her greens on time or consuming raw smoothies. But the moment she combined a healthy nutrition programme which consisted of vegetables and good fats with yoga, suddenly, the toxins lodged inside her started expelling. This beautiful young woman has reversed her PCOS diagnosis and the symptoms that remain are also disappearing fast.

Women with PCOS, the most common hormone imbalance in women of reproductive age, may be more vulnerable to exposure to BPA, found in many plastic household items as per multiple researches globally.[12] And yet, we continue to feed babies in plastic bottles with warm milk, the temperature of the milk in itself leeches the BPA on to the milk they drink. We may not have a solution for the leached plastic entering our body, but we definitely have a solution for how to remove it.

We are not only body, we are not only mind. We are holistic beings. How we respond to our environment is what makes us healthy or unhealthy. When there are so many toxins inside us and our response to stress is poor, our anxiety levels are higher; these toxins can lodge themselves and form colonies inside our gut or other parts of the body. Pregnant women who are highly exposed to common environmental chemicals—polyfluoroalkyl compounds (PFCs)—have babies that are smaller at birth and larger at 20 months of age, according to a new study. PFCs are used in the production of fluoropolymers and are found widely in protective coatings of packaging products, clothes, furniture and non-stick cookware. They are persistent compounds found abundantly in the environment and human exposure is common. PFCs have been detected in human sera, breast milk and cord blood.[13]

Now let's talk baby boys. Doctors and researchers know that man-made chemicals commonly found in plastics, foods, personal care products and building materials can interfere with how hormones like oestrogen and testosterone work in the body. A study by Seattle Children's Hospital[14] showed a clear connection between a pregnant woman's exposure to the endocrine-disrupting (ED) chemical called DEHP and subsequent anomalies in a baby boy's reproductive organs. This association was discovered by collecting urine samples from pregnant women and testing them for phthalates and doing physical exams of newborns.

While doctors and researchers have known that ED chemicals interfere with hormones, it has been difficult to prove clear health outcomes. Now, for the first time, we've shown that the higher the DEHP concentration in a mother's urine, the more likely her boy would be born with a genital anomaly.

As a result, a lot of boys are facing hormonal fluctuations and issues and it is a topic not discussed often.

The good news is that you can live a life where you can enjoy good health and continue to detox on a regular basis as part of your lifestyle. The permanent solution is in going inwards and understanding your body and mind, working with it rather than against it. Without understanding the biochemical processes inside, the stress triggers, the clinical reports, incorporating a healthy lifestyle that has a regular detox element inbuilt, becomes impossible.

In the next chapter, we try to understand and customize your own detox programme, something that is sustainable and empowers to achieve good health, high energy, positivity and a glowing skin!

Chapter 2

21 Signs Your Body Has a Toxin Build-Up

You know the obvious signs when you feel you need a detox. Or do you? Most people will go on a detox plan just to lose weight or get rid of acne. But weight loss and clear skin are just a few effects of cleansing yourself and if you cannot carry through the detox, the acne will return. As you saw in the case of Meghana, a combination of a poor immune system due to preterm birth, followed by excessive bottle feeding led to endocrine disruptors lodging inside her delicate body. Before puberty and during puberty, signs of these endocrine disruptors became obvious. Unidimensional treatments were unsuccessful. What helped her was a long-term nurturing programme which has now become a *way of life* for her. What has worked for Meghana may not work for you. So let us dive deep into understanding your symptoms and helping you devise your own healthy lifestyle where you self-nurture and release toxins on a regular basis.

21 SIGNS OF TOXINS

1. You eat large meals—it could be just one meal a day but it is large.
2. You like your food artificially spicy (use of packet masalas,

sauces) as you do not enjoy the natural flavours of vegetables.
3. You are dependent on caffeine—tea or coffee. You must have it every day otherwise it leads to headaches or lack of freshness.
4. Your stomach is not always okay—constipation, diarrhoea and bloating trouble you and you cannot pinpoint exactly what food is causing this.
5. You get frequent skin breakouts.
6. You are irritable without reason.
7. You experience hair fall.
8. You have period-related problems—irregular periods, painful with spasms, PMS, mood swings and/or breast tenderness.
9. You get headaches at least two or three times in a month.
10. Your energy levels are poor even after eight hours of sleep.
11. You have unexplained pains or muscle aches.
12. Your gums feel swollen or itchy a few times a month.
13. You have sensitive teeth.
14. You get frequent colds, coughs, flu or low-grade fever.
15. You are diabetic.
16. You have high cholesterol.
17. You have brain fog or frequent forgetfulness.
18. Your physical body balance is poor.
19. You have difficulty losing weight.
20. You drink more than three times a week, or you drink twice a month but indulge in binge drinking.
21. You smoke or consume tobacco or live with somebody who consumes tobacco/smokes.

So how much did you get? If you think five or more of these apply to you, means you need to read this book carefully.

And what will happen if you don't follow a detox plan?

Let's look at the above signs and connect them to the health problems you could experience in the future if you ignore detoxing yourself.

1. **Eating large meals.** I know many people who eat only once a day but that meal is large. The definition of large is that they will have a portion of rice, two rotis, a bowl of dal, a bowl of vegetables, one papad, some pickle and definitely a small sweet at the end of the meal. Visually, if you look at their plate or Thali, it is fairly full. There is less empty space. The logic that such people give is that they are eating only once a day. But the human body is not made to hoard food in the stomach like camels hold water in their body. We are meant to nourish frequently throughout the day and eat small quantities for our digestive system and liver to perform efficiently. A large meal consisting of more carbohydrates will send all the energy to the digestive system and make it difficult to absorb nutrients as well as release toxins. The kinds of combination I have listed above are also very heavy and difficult to digest. This makes the release of toxins even more problematic, leading to many more symptoms of toxicity as listed below. Most people who eat large meals also experience some of the other symptoms like headaches, sluggishness, lack of freshness, constipation, bloating and, often, difficulty losing weight, especially for women.
2. **Spicy food.** Eating spicy food is not a problem if you do it occasionally. But when you add chutneys, pickles, sauces, packet masalas on a regular basis, meal after meal, you are making the stomach environment acidic. Also, it often demonstrates that you have lost touch with the natural flavours of the food and hence need to dunk it

in masala, chillies and other spices. Mostly, spicy food is also a sign of overcooked food which means that the food has completely lost all the nutrients in the process of overcooking.

3. **You are dependent on caffeine.** When our energy is not high or brain is not fresh, our dependency on tea or coffee is much higher. Lack of freshness indicates higher toxin levels. Consuming too much caffeine via these two beverages or other aerated drinks like colas and energy drinks which also have high caffeine, can lead to stripping of the digestive tract and poor absorption of nutrients.

4. **Your stomach is not always okay.** Poor digestion usually means that your hormones are fluctuating, and you have difficulty absorbing nutrients from food. When you absorb some nutrients, these are insufficient in reaching the various organs and performing the functions that the body and mind needs in order to stay healthy. In that scenario, low immunity sets in.

5. **Frequent skin breakouts.** Not having flawless skin can be a traumatic life experience. But that is not all. Skin breakouts like acne, eczema and psoriasis are linked to a poor gut and can develop into autoimmune responses which are difficult to treat with medicines alone. Acne is a clear sign of fluctuating hormones and a weak gut.

6. **You are irritable.** When there are higher levels of toxins and low nutrient absorption, our mood is mostly off. Especially for people who remember being happy-go-lucky when they were younger, the current environment, stress and work overload is only part of the problem. With fluctuating hormones like cortisol, serotonin, oxytocin and poor intake of nutrients for the brain, irritability is a clear sign of a toxin overload blocking absorption of

nutrients required for brain calmness.

7. **You experience hair fall.** Heavy metal poisoning usually causes brittle hair and hair loss and often goes undetected. Many medications like steroids and chemotherapy drugs prescribed to patients with immuno-compromised health issues (some of them listed in the previous chapter) trigger hair fall and brittle hair. Continuous hair fall will lead to baldness and a poor nutritional status. Less hair on the head will make you look older than you are. And just the stress of losing hair is enough for many people to experience accelerated anxiety, poor self-esteem and/or low moods—all of which create stomach acids and strip the digestive system.

8. **Your energy levels are low even after eight hours of sleep.** This means that the quality of your sleep is poor. An agitated brain can cause this. You need energy to work towards your dreams. With chronic fatigue and lack of freshness comes poor decision-making. A detoxified body and mind are always calm, fresh and energetic, ready to take on the world.

9. **Period problems.** These are a sign of hormonal fluctuations, PCOS and can cause infertility. Heavy periods, dysmenorrhea—pain during or before periods—breast tenderness, mood swings, acne breakouts a week before the periods and/or stubborn weight are all signs of period problems. And all the hormonal storms most young women are facing are due to endocrine disruptors in our environment and food chain. When we cleanse ourselves, these disruptors get released, leading to a higher quality of life.

10. **You get headaches.** Consider this tiresome cycle: your sleep is poor, due to this you are not fresh, digestion is

poor, sleep is less or disturbed. Less or disturbed sleep can also cause constipation. All these factors lead to frequent headaches.

11. **Your gums feel swollen or itchy a few times a month.** Signs of inflammation and a compromised gut usually start in the form of swollen gums. If you have these symptoms, you need to detoxify your gut and reduce inflammation levels by switching to an anti-inflammatory lifestyle, which we will discuss later in the book.

12. **You have sensitive teeth.** Tooth sensitivity is because of the upset balance in our gut. Our digestive enzymes start in our mouth and when there is an acidic balance in your gut, it will reflect in the form of tooth sensitivity. A superficial method to douse this tooth sensitivity with medicated toothpaste is a temporary solution. The root cause is the acids in your stomach which are because of high levels of physical or emotional toxins.

13. **You have unexplained pains.** This is a sign of inflammation, too many preservatives, too much mucous formation in the body. Pain levels increase due to the toxins blocking absorption of nutrients. When the minerals in our synovial fluid decrease and we cannot absorb nutrients from food because of high toxic load, lack of nutrients in the synovial fluid cause joint pain. It can also lead to damaged nerves and cause nerve pain. Continuous periods of chronic pain lead to chronic fatigue and brain fog. Getting rid of unexplained pains is so much easier with an anti-inflammatory lifestyle that expels toxins on a regular basis, and make space for nutrients to be absorbed by your body.

14. **You get frequent colds, coughs, flu or low-grade fever.** This evidently means that your immunity is low and you

are at risk for catching all kinds of viruses—including the COVID-19 virus.

15. **You are diabetic.** Excess levels of sugar in your body are toxins you need to release immediately. Excess sugar damages the nerves, eyes, kidneys and increases risk of cancer.
16. **You have high cholesterol.** High bad lipids increase your risk of various diseases—inviting heart disease, anxiety, depression, memory loss, increased risk for Alzheimer's and Parkinson's. Getting rid of bad cholesterol and high triglycerides is imperative in order to reduce the risk of these and other treatable conditions. High bad lipids could also be a sign of a fatty liver which means that your liver is not detoxifying at the rate at which it should.
17. **You have brain fog.** A high number of toxins can cause brain fog, which is identified by feeling dazed, forgetting things and wanting to rest often. This can reduce efficiency at home or at work, make response to relationships poor, leading to frequent relationship conflicts.
18. **Your balance is poor.** High toxins will create an imbalance in your spine and body, leading to frequent falls, poor balance and a feeling of dizziness. This can lead to injury and put you at high risk for spine-related issues. Among older adults, a poor body balance is usually the first sign for an increased risk of neurodegenerative diseases like dementia and Alzheimer's. A simple test for this is if you can stand on one leg for more than 20 seconds, your body balance is good. If not, it increases your risk of cognitive decline.
19. **You have difficulty losing weight.** Obesity is a risk factor for heart disease, type two diabetes, PCOS and cancer. If you have difficulty losing weight, following a detoxification

lifestyle programme is going to help you not just lose weight and experience higher energy but also reduce the risk of all these deadly diseases.
20. **Alcohol.** Of course, we all enjoy an occasional glass of wine and it is healthy too! However, excess alcohol in the body puts pressure on the liver and strips the stomach lining. It also makes you gain weight, increases inflammation levels and puts your heart at risk. Excess alcohol has been linked to esophagus, neck and head cancers.
21. **Tobacco use.** This is probably the only toxin in the universe that has universal agreement on zero benefits. Unlike alcohol, which if consumed in small quantities, has certain health benefits, tobacco use has no benefits. Tobacco will raise your cholesterol, put your heart at risk, increase the risk of different kinds of cancers, suppress the immune system and in case you have been diagnosed with cancer, make recovery very difficult.

If you still need convincing to adapt to a lifestyle that follows the principles of detox, here's the truth: wouldn't you want fresh energy and beautiful glowing skin? Now that I have your attention, let's understand how to do this!

Chapter 3

Why My Shuddha Programme Works

The human body is extraordinary. There is the physical aspect of it being a machine and performing daily activities, and then there is consciousness and self-awareness. What medical science today understands is only the physical level and not the consciousness and self-awareness level. A combination of our mind and body functioning in unison helps us regenerate ourselves. Just look at the illustration below:

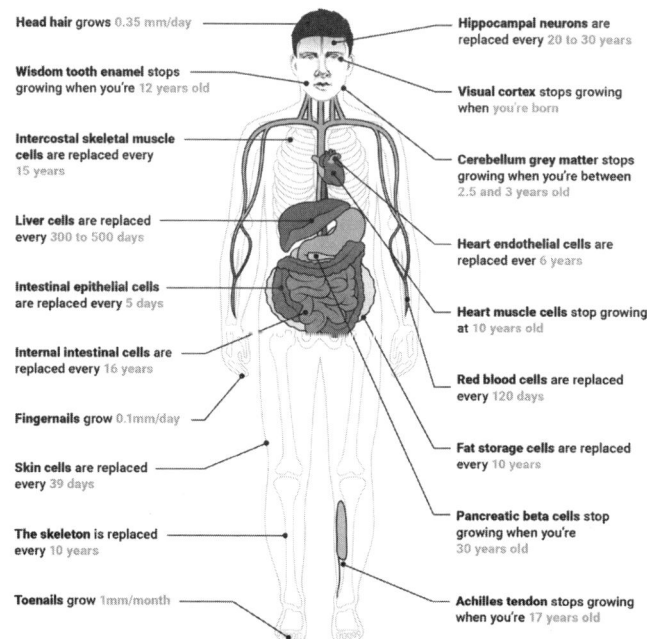

We are designed to grow, repair and regenerate. That is evident when we watch a little baby growing up, our nails growing, our hair growing, a cut healing or a bone joining back together. When we get a skin rash, the skin heals and new cells replace the old ones and skin texture improves once the rash has disappeared. This is because we are shedding dead skin cells constantly. Cells that make up your skin are replaced every two to three weeks. As the primary protection against the external environment, your skin is the biggest organ that demonstrates the state of toxins inside you. Your outer layer of skin, the epidermis (apart from the thicker dermis beneath), replaces itself every 35 days. When this process of dead skin cells shedding and being replaced by new cells becomes slow, it is either due to age, lifestyle and presence of toxins or accelerated ageing due to disease. These toxins could be physical or emotional.

Other parts of the body also regenerate as listed below:[15]

1. A human liver can regenerate completely even if as little as 25 per cent of it remains.
2. Your stomach lining replaces itself every four days.
3. The stomach cells that come into contact with food are replaced every five minutes.
4. Our entire skeletal structures are regenerated every three months.
5. Cells that line your stomach can renew as fast as every two days, since they're often in contact with digestive acid.
6. White blood cells, the main heroes in fighting infections, can last from a few days to a little over a week. Red blood cells last for about four months.
7. Fat cells live longer (yes, unfortunately!)—an average age of 10 years.

8. The bones in your body also regenerate about every 10 years.
9. Cells in your hippocampus (part of the brain)—the part responsible for memory—can regrow.

If we want this regeneration process to be efficient, the release of old cells and dead cells needs to be on a continuous basis. And this continuous basis is the lifestyle we are talking about in this book. The cycle of life to continuously cleanse yourself to avoid diseases and have strong immunity begins with a sustainable detox plan.

To be shuddha then becomes your primary health goal.

As you are aware, the simple meaning of shuddha is pure. And it is this purity that we all seek for our mind and body to live the content life. A content life means feeling the best we can every single day of our lives.

The reason why my Shuddha programme works in the above context is because of the following:

1. **It reactivates the natural rhythm inside you.** Each one of us is born with a natural rhythm. We respond well to stability and structure. This stability and structure is a natural flowing process, never still. According to Ayurveda, this is the rhythm that heals. To give you an example, we are comfortable in a predictable environment—the sun rises every morning and we take that for granted. So for us the sun is a stabilizing factor because it is predictable. However, the sun is not just there, stationary. The sun is also moving around the centre of the Milky Way along with the entire solar system; one complete orbit will take about 230 million years.[16] The sun is in constant motion just like the Earth. It does not rise, as it is the Earth that moves around it. But because we have become comfortable

with the rhythm and structure of the sun rising every day, we feel comforted in the predictability of the soothing sunrise.

Just like nature has a rhythm, so does our body. Even when we are sitting, the cells in our body are in constant motion, like the Earth and the sun are. But at the outward physical level, it seems like we are still. This internal rhythm, when disturbed, prevents our body from performing the job it knows best—to repair itself. When we move away from this rhythm, we start having health problems. The time we sleep, the time we wake up, the time we eat, are all important times for our body to absorb nutrients, expel toxins and help us repair and restore our balance. Sleeping extremely late, skipping breakfast, eating heavy or imbalanced meals, disrupt that natural rhythm. When we start on any health programme, its biggest success comes from the consistency and rhythm of doing it every day, day after day, just like the rising sun. In my programme, as you will see in your four phases of cleansing yourself to become shuddha, you will initially not feel like doing those things. However, when you set a rhythm to it, after 30 days you will want to continue with those new habits you are forming. These new habits will become the foundation of your new rhythm that will help you stay healthy.

2. **It repairs your gut.** The human body and mind are very complex. The gut microbe is everywhere. Just like toxins. Medical science has discovered toxins in each and every part of our body. There are toxins in our enzymes, toxins that leach onto our arteries and stick there, there are toxins in our gut which obstruct absorption of nutrients, emotional toxins we carry as burdens which cause physical

ramifications of anxiety, acidity, stress and hypertension. When released, they make space for good health. If you look at various scientific studies, our gut microbe is not just in our gut, this good or bad bacteria is in every tissue. It has been found in the breast tissue for breast cancer patients and in the brain tissue for brain tumour patients. Hence, the way to release toxins is to change your gut microbe.

The shuddha programme repairs the gut via infesting it with the good bacteria which kills the bad bacteria and the digestive system expels this as waste. Till we do not repair our gut, the release of toxins is not possible. This programme goes to each and every part of your mind and body to grab these toxins and releases them completely from your digestive system on a continuous basis. And then, when we combine this continuous rhythm of eating at specific times with the right kind of nutrients, along with the activities and exercises given in the next few chapters, the holistic manner in which toxins get released is unique and complete.

3. **It restores your balance.** Once the gut is clean and mind and body are in balance, there is no place for toxicity. Suddenly, after 60 days of being on my shuddha programme, you will realize that your response to stress has changed, it is calmer, but all you changed was how you ate and lived, you did not do any therapy or counselling. And yet, because of this restored balance, your mind discovered its own flow and rhythm without any hurry. Unhurried decisions are always more sound and responsible. You will also see that your digestive system is performing more efficiently and your skin has begun to get that glow. A lot of women who undergo

my shuddha programme are asked if they have got work done on their skin because their skin is naturally glowing with good health even though they have lost weight. With other detox programmes many people feel fatigue, lack of nourishment, dry skin, wrinkles, brittle hair or hair fall. However, with my programme, once you finish with the four steps, you will only feel re-energized and restored in your mind and body balance, which will be evident in your calm state of mind, glowing skin and sound sleep.

And what happens when you incorporate this restorative balance in your daily life?

Chapter 4

Preparing for a Holistically Shuddha Life

Planning is everything! When we plan well for any event in our life, the event goes off smoothly. Planning for your shuddha programme will also ensure that you do not face any impediments in cleansing yourself and leading a wonderful life ahead.

There must be many signs you would find in yourself for needing a detox. You could simply do it to lose weight, or you could be feeling a toxin load through some of the symptoms I have listed earlier. Incorporating a lifestyle that detoxes is a step-by-step process and helps you lead a healthy life. It releases excess weight and toxins which do not come back, and this is easier than you have been made to believe.

Your holistic detox plan is not just going to focus on expelling temporary toxins, it is also going to focus on first getting you to be healthier and then living that healthier life on a daily basis. And that is why my holistic detox plan has four steps, which I call my four Rs.

1. Repair the gut
2. Release the toxins
3. Reactivate your rhythm
4. Restore your balance

For each step, you will come across various recipes and guidelines which may seem like they have nothing to do with the food you ingest, but they will help you detoxify yourself. Many foods are initially eliminated because they will hinder the detox journey. You need to be completely prepared before you start deep diving into your clean future. It is this future that is going to help you get higher immunity, glowing skin and a disease-free, high-energy life. So how do you prepare? Here are simple steps to stock up and warm up your mind for your beautiful journey ahead.

Move the impediments out. Like I have mentioned above, we cannot make way for nutrients to get absorbed if we have the presence of toxins all around us. So the first step is to get rid of whatever can entice us into becoming weak during our detox process. These are:

1. All packet foods in your kitchen cupboard
2. Packet masalas
3. Alcohol
4. Tobacco in any form
5. Caffeine
6. Animal protein
7. Sour items
8. Wheat and white flour
9. Clutter in your home

All packet foods in your kitchen cupboard. An absence of these in your home is going to reduce your temptation to falter in your detox plan to heal yourself. All these carry toxins. You already know that packet foods are unhealthy for you. This is so because they use refried oil, or unhealthy oils, which we have already discussed in the previous chapter. They also have a lot of preservatives and additives to maintain the crispness and flavour intact which can strip your gut and reduce absorption of nutrients. In addition, many have preservatives and artificial colouring, which increases allergies and inflammation and destroys your gut bacteria. Destruction of gut microbe by these chemicals helps them make colonies in your body, and these sites can help tumours grow.[17] So, out they all go!

Packet masalas. These are another source of toxins. Most packet masalas are mixed in factory settings where hygiene conditions are suspect. On top of that, there are fillers used which are not good for our digestive tract. According to studies conducted by Pesticide Residue Research and Analysis Laboratory under the Kerala Agricultural University, spices like coriander, dried ginger powder, dried red chilli, cardamom, cumin powder, pickle powder, garam masala, curd chilli, chilli powder, fennel seeds, Kashmiri chilli powder, rasam powder and curry powder available in the market are laced with toxic chemicals. Two hundred and eighty-five samples of spices, masala powders and processed foods were tested from supermarkets in Kerala. And 38 samples presented contaminants exceeding permitted limits prescribed by the European Union.[18]

So what were the contaminants? Endosulfan residue was found in samples of coriander. Endosulfan is a pesticide which is being phased out globally. It was used widely on crops like cashew, cotton, tea, paddy, fruits and others until 2011, when the Supreme Court banned its production and distribution. The health effects of this toxic chemical include neurotoxicity, late sexual maturity, physical deformities and poisoning, among others. People, especially newborns, have suffered deformities, health complications and loss of family members due to exposure to this agrochemical.[19]

Samples of jeera were found to be contaminated with hazardous pesticides like chlorpyrifos, ethion, malathion, methyl parathion and profenofos, all considered harmful to humans as per the WHO. Dried chilly had residue from chlorpyrifos, sypermethrin, lambda cyhalothrin and cunalfos. The Consumer Education and Research Centre (CERC) study found presence of heavy metals beyond the safe limits in leading brands of organic turmeric powder.[20][21]

CERC tested six popular national organic turmeric powder brands for safety, namely, lead, copper, tin, zinc, cadmium, arsenic and mercury. Of the six brands tested, none were found to have chemicals or lead or tin. Mercury and cadmium were within limits, but copper and arsenic were found in the organic spices. Long-term exposure to arsenic in food can cause cancer, heart disease, diabetes and other diseases. The US Food and Drug Administration (FDA) reported 12 per cent of spices imported into the United States were contaminated with insect parts, whole insects, rodent hairs, etc., according to an analysis of spice imports by the FDA.[22]

American authorities also found nearly seven per cent spice imports to be contaminated with salmonella, a toxic bacteria that can cause severe illness. Spice imports from India and Mexico were found to have the highest rate of contamination.

So just throw packet masalas out. Flavour can come from many other clean sources, as you will discover later in this book!

Tobacco and alcohol. We don't need to discuss the toxic effects of tobacco, so I will get straight down to why alcohol needs to be out. Alcohol-induced bacteria destroys and interferes with liver detoxification. During any detoxification programme, our liver plays the most important role and presence of alcohol is going to compromise your liver function and disrupt the detoxification of the toxins inside you.

Animal protein. Most vegetarians think that they are healthy because they do not consume animal protein, forgetting that milk and milk products are animal protein. Milk is an inflammatory food and can increase mucus in the body which can destroy your gut, increase inflammation levels and increase bad lipids like cholesterol and triglycerides. Please do remember that the fat in milk is saturated fat. On top of that, milk comes from an animal and carries the natural hormones of the cow or buffalo. Even if you are having organic milk, the natural hormones will be present and they will become endocrine disruptors and cause hormonal issues in women and young girls. At this stage, when we are trying to expel the toxins and pacify the hormones, having even a very small quantity of any milk product including yoghurt is going to derail your detoxification programme. In phase three, when you are restoring your balance, this will be added back in small quantities.

Sour items. Foods like lemon and lime have been touted as wonderful detoxification foods. However, when your gut is already acidic, presence of any sour items can upset this balance completely. We first need to pacify the gut and nurture it. After that, we can add these back in small quantities. The problem with sour items is also that it erodes your tooth enamel and causes bone pain. For most people who come to me requiring a detox, also exhibit symptoms of unexplained pains. A pure detoxification programme should not include anything sour such as lime, lemon, vinegar, tomatoes, tamarind or any other form of sour items. This is mandatory to be removed because it can upset the entire balance of healing at this stage. It will be incorporated back in small quantities at a later stage.

Wheat. Wheat, white flour and gluten in any form, are only a form of genetically modified seeds. Gluten does not get broken down and hence leeches on to our digestive tracts, causing a leaky gut. This leaky gut can trigger allergies, autoimmune conditions and compromised immunity. It also stops the absorption of nutrients. Hence, your wholewheat rotis are of no use and will not be healthy at this point in time. Then what is healthy? I have a whole section of recipes later in the book to help you with that!

Clutter. Having a congested home blocks the flow of positive energy, leading to blocked negative energy. And negative energy is a toxin. Remove some of your furniture, donate the clothes that you have not used for one year and throw away cosmetics and perishables that you have not used for a while. Hoarding or accumulating is a sign of feeling emotionally unsettled and as you will discover in Part Three of this book. Emotional heaviness is as big a toxin as having poor eating habits. This is an important aspect of sanitizing your outer space. In the entire detox plan, we are looking at sanitizing our inner space in our bodies but if the space outside where we live is still full of clutter, we will be visually seeing and reabsorbing the same way of living that had pushed us towards the accumulation of these toxins.

Our entire purpose for the detoxification programme is to remove the toxins and make way for a clean lifestyle that will not block well-being.

PHASE ONE: REPAIR THE GUT—PREPARATION

Now that you have understood what all to throw out, for the first phase of your detoxification programme, where you are going to expel the toxins gently while nurturing your digestive system to repair it, below is the list of items required.

These ingredients are going to be the base for all the yummy recipes that you will read later in my book. Without these ingredients, your gut will not get cleansed and positivity will not start setting in. Hence, it is very important for you to stock up on the following:

1. **Oxygenating plants.** When you declutter your home, you realize that there is a lot of space to breathe and for positive energy to move. Fill up some of this space with indoor plants like areca palm that are natural air purifiers. This plant is very commonly available at all nurseries as well as online and is not very expensive; it also looks very beautiful. The siblings of areca palm—lady palm and bamboo palm—are also effective and look equally charming. Apart from these, rubber plant, Dracaena, philodendron and the Boston fern are easily available locally and are easy to maintain. These plants will, during the day, increase the level of oxygen in your home, thereby leading to a faster recovery process. The pandemic situation has also helped us understand the importance of an oxygenated body and mind for our survival. Doing the breath work that I have prescribed in the later part of the book in the presence of these plants, will enhance oxygen levels more efficiently and the release of toxins and free radicals will be faster.
2. **Aloe vera plant.** An aloe vera plant is extremely cost-effective with multiple benefits. It is one of the few plants

that gives us oxygen 24 hours of the day and can be put into your bedroom without any problems. While you sleep, it gives you enough oxygen and heals you. The other benefits of aloe vera are for the skin and gut. It is an essential part of the detoxification programme that you have an aloe vera plant in your home. I would strongly recommend that you invest in three plants because you can use one and when it is completely cut, you can move to the second and third one. By the time you have finished with the third aloe vera plant, the first plant would have already grown substantially again. Between three plants, you can rotate your entire aloe vera needs.

3. **Green tea.** The gut pacifying and anti-inflammatory properties of green tea are well known. They kill bad bacteria and are potently anti-cancer because they kill the bad cells in the body and release toxins. Green tea leaves are the most potent beverage clinically proven to have healing benefits. When combined as per the recipes I have given in the meal plan, with other natural ingredients, green tea becomes even more potent in the detoxification process.

4. **Chamomile tea.** Chamomile is a medicinal plant used mainly in the treatment of stomach and intestinal diseases. It has therapeutic properties and helps in enhancing our heart health, reducing type two diabetes symptoms and repairing the gut. In our journey of cleansing ourselves, repair of the gut is critical and so is consumption of this beautiful herb tea to repair the gut and help us sleep well. These leaves have medicinal powers to relax and calm us and stimulate sound sleep. Consume it as guided in the next part.

5. **Organic honey.** It has the power to infuse natural

probiotics and minerals to repair the gut. Unlike modern-day honeys which are adulterated with sugar, organic honey, when taken in small quantities, is beneficial. The hallmark of organic honey is that it does not solidify or change colour when it is refrigerated. If you look at any of the mass produced modern-day honey bottles, when you put them in the refrigerator, they become thicker. This does not happen with real organic honey. This way you can tell the difference between adulterated and unadulterated honey.

6. **Extra virgin olive oil.** Benefits of this unsaturated fat are humongous. Apart from cleansing and pacifying your gut, extra virgin olive oil also reduces inflammation levels in the body, expels out bad fats by sticking on to the bad fat, loosening it and expelling it through your gut. It is also proven to be heart protective and brain protective and wards off against high cholesterol, fatty liver, high triglycerides, neurodegenerative diseases, hormonal issues and pain-related issues. With so many benefits, the presence of extra virgin olive oil in the recipes and quantities given later in my book is absolutely essential to your detoxification programme. Always look for a glass bottle, and it should say cold pressed or cold extracted somewhere on the bottle. This is the only expensive ingredient for your detoxification programme. I have seen higher benefits of extra virgin olive oil versus any other cold pressed oils like flaxseed oil. While virgin flaxseed oil is amazing for balancing hormones, in a detoxification programme, extra virgin olive oil is much more efficient. At a later stage in life, you can add flaxseed oil but in the first phase your fat should only come from extra virgin olive oil.

7. **Moong dal.** The only lentil allowed during the detoxification process is moong dal. While normally you would have heard all lentils and pulses are beneficial, moong dal comes with some unique properties. It has high polyphenols,[23] which are clinically proven to improve digestion, brain function and heart health. What is most amazing about moong dal is that unlike other lentils and pulses, it does not cause mucus in the body. All other lentils and pulses can get acidic in the gut, hence destroying the process of detoxification and gut repair. However, moong dal is gut pacifying and healing. It is used extensively in Ayurveda, not only for detoxification programmes but also on an everyday basis to provide the right kind of fibre, protein and minerals. Try and source organic moong dal, it is easily available across many online platforms.
8. **Brown rice.** Just like not all calories are created equal, not all carbohydrates are created equal. The mineral and fibre which is stripped from white rice is naturally present in wild brown rice. Brown rice and white rice are from the same crop but have a different process of cleansing. White rice is polished and cleansed of fibre while brown rice is not refined as much. Hence it contains many of the minerals and vitamins as well as fibre which were stripped in the process of polishing to convert to white rice. It is available in every corner of the country and is usually referred to as unrefined, coarse, desi or *mota chawal*. The gut pacifying benefits as well as trace minerals that repair the gut are abundantly present in brown rice. It takes a longer time to cook and hence should always be cooked in the pressure cooker. Soaking it overnight is going to destroy the water-soluble minerals and vitamins in brown rice. Stock up on this

wonder carbohydrate and use it as per meal plans and recipes listed later in the book.

9. **Flattened rice (poha).** The benefits of this gentle and calming carbohydrate in pacifying the gut are many. Even when I treat chronic disease patients ravaged by medicines and diseases and with very low absorption of nutrients, the simple poha or flattened rice, a common breakfast or snack item in Maharashtra, Gujarat and Madhya Pradesh, is extremely beneficial to anybody with toxins and gut issues. The gentility of this preparation is indispensable in nurturing your digestive tract back to good health. Make sure to purchase thick poha that is readily available in Indian grocery stores or online. Also stock up on the thin variety, for making chivda for phase two. Thin poha is best used for chivda, a yummy crunchy snack.

10. **Organic peanuts.** Peanuts are wonderful for garnishing and have nutrients and healing ingredients. They have good fats and protein and technically they are legumes. They reduce sugar spikes in the bloodstream and hence a small quantity of these are ideal for those with obesity or type two diabetes. Since they are also cheaply available, anybody can source organic peanuts and does not need to look for expensive options of nuts if those are not affordable. However, most peanuts that we get in the market are not organic and have a toxin known as aflatoxin which can damage the liver. If you can get organic peanuts, these are required in small quantities during the detox and later. Do not exceed quantities listed in the recipes.

11. **Weekly list of vegetables.** The purpose of vegetables in the detoxification programme as well as in restoring your balance is extremely critical. Vegetables not only repair

the gut and penetrate the digestive system and your entire body with good gut bacteria, they also are very powerful antioxidants and repair everything that has gone wrong with you till then. For example, many women come to me with excessive hair fall and all I do is ask them to increase their vegetable intake. And suddenly, their hair stops falling, and new hair growth begins. This also leads to reduced pigmentation and reduces acne flare-ups for them and they start looking younger very quickly without any procedures. Wherever you live, there are always seasonal vegetables available. Potatoes and paneer are not vegetables! Please stock up on a large variety of seasonal vegetables with the following quantities and planning in mind:

a. ***Three vegetables per day.*** This will mean that you will need to stock up on different varieties of vegetables. You can repeat vegetables two or three times a week but not more. The more variety you eat, the better it is for you to detox your gut and release all the toxins inside. Rotating vegetables, ensuring that every meal you eat has both green and red/orange colours is extremely important. For example, in one meal, have fenugreek leaves, carrots and bottle gourd. The second meal can have red or yellow peppers, spinach and ridge gourd. Always combine heavy to digest vegetables like fenugreek or cauliflower or cabbage with one of the gourds, which is easier on the gut. During the first phase, more light vegetables will be part of the recipes. As your gut starts the repair process, the combinations will become more interesting!

b. ***Garnishes and salads.*** Onions, ginger, garlic and cucumber are crucial for garnishing and cleansing in any detoxification programme. Purchase these at the start of the week so that you never run out of them.

c. ***Herbs.*** Fresh coriander, curry leaves or kadi patta (one of my favourites), celery and mint are available in most vegetable markets throughout the year. Keep a ready stock of these as you will require them for the recipes during your detoxification process.

d. ***Wash all items properly.*** Wash everything, first with tap water, then with drinking water. For leaves (including fresh herbs for garnishing and flavour, such as coriander and mint), wash well with tap water, soak in tap water with one tablespoon sea salt or Himalayan salt dissolved in a large pan for five minutes, drain, soak in drinking water with one tablespoon salt dissolved in the pan for five minutes, then drain and consume. This strips the pesticides and any infectious bacteria away. Even for organic vegetables and leaves, it is necessary to do this. You want to ensure that you only get the clean and healing benefits of all the vegetables. Hence, when you purchase these vegetables on a weekly basis, finish this activity and store them in the fridge so that when you take out any item, you know that you have already made them hygienic and healthy.

e. ***Pre-cut in the morning.*** Yes, of course, it is preferable if you cut fresh vegetables and then prepare a dish. However, if you do not have the luxury to do that, you can cut all your vegetables in one go and put them in the refrigerator.

12. **Stock up on rice bran oil.** Even though your usage of oil is going to be minimal, rice bran oil is the safest option at this stage. Rice bran oil blocks the absorption of bad

cholesterol,[24] which is a bad fat and is a toxin in the body. It has a high flame point and hence makes it safe for tempering, tadka and seasoning.

13. **Organic spices.** Stock up on the following organic spices and use them as per the meal plan and recipes given later in the book. These are absolutely essential for expelling all the excess bad bacteria, toxins, viruses and sugar from the body.
   a. Turmeric
   b. Cloves
   c. Cardamom
   d. Cinnamon
   e. Aniseed
   f. Pepper
   g. Fennel
   h. Methi seeds
   i. Mustard seeds
   j. Cumin seeds
   k. Himalayan or sea salt

A note on organic produce: Companies such as Organic India, 24 Mantra Organic, Conscious Food and Satva Organic are some of the organic products companies that sell online. Please remember that in India, guidelines for organic foods are not very well defined by the government and the Food Safety and Standards Authority of India (FSSAI). Even though maximum residue limits have been defined by the FSSAI organic certification, many of these limits are in lesser detail than in other developed nations. Additionally, testing of organic products is not frequent in India. This is evident because the same packet masalas that have FSSAI approval were rejected by the FDA in the US. Hence, you will have to do your research and ensure that the organic brand that you choose also grows its produce in organic soil. Our soil is full of pesticides, chemicals, pollutants, arsenic, lead and other heavy metals. Some of the organic companies first clean up this soil and then plant the vegetables.

PHASE TWO: RELEASE THE TOXINS— PREPARATION

In phase two, there are a few more items added. The items from phase one will continue to be present as part of your detoxification programme, however, the following also need to be stocked up in this phase.

Quinoa/Oats. Both these wonderful carbohydrates are rich in fibre and proteins and are required in phase two to continue the detoxification programme. As per availability in your city or town, you can access any one of these. They cannot be added in phase one because they are a little difficult to digest if you have a compromised gut and in the first phase our entire focus is on gently nurturing the digestive system to repair itself in order to not only expel the toxins but also start having the ability to absorb nutrients from food. We cannot have any impediments to that and hence difficult to digest carbohydrates should not be added in phase one, strictly. Many people believe that millets are healthy, which may be true when you are completely in harmony with your mind, body and soul and your gut is healed, but during the phase of repair, millets are extremely heavy to digest and can completely derail the journey of your detox. Stay away from any other carbohydrates except what is listed here in a step-by-step manner.

Snack items: Stock up on thin poha required to make chivda, makhanas (fox nuts) and/or murmura (puffed rice). Quantities and recipes will be given in the recipes section for this phase.

Specific fruits. In phase one, we strictly cannot have any form of sugar, even if it is natural sugar. It is a given that you will have viruses and fungus in your body and any form of sugar feeds on these. Hence, even healing fruits should be added only in phase two. The only fruits that are added at this stage are apple, muskmelon, pomegranate, pineapple, red grapes, black grapes, wild berries or jamun, papaya and all kinds of berries. As per availability in your city or town, you can choose any three fruits, plus papaya. Consumption of papaya is mandatory in phase two.

Specific nuts and seeds. In phase one, nuts and seeds can irritate the gut and become an impediment to the digestive nurturing we want to achieve. However, now, when your gut is pacified, addition of this beautiful vegan protein becomes extremely crucial. Nuts and seeds are also a good source of good fat which gets destroyed if you roast them. And good unsaturated fat has multiple benefits as we have already discussed. Along with that, seeds have an adequate quantity of protein required for muscle functioning and for reducing fatigue. Please stock up on Mamra almonds, salted pistachios, chia seeds and walnuts. You can use them as per the meal plan and recipes listed for phase two.

PHASE THREE: RESTORE THE BALANCE— PREPARATION

By the time you reach this phase, much of the repair work would have happened and you would have seen the benefits of the detoxification programme. Now it is time to incorporate this programme into your daily lives rather than subjecting your mind and body to harsh short-term detoxes. All the ingredients listed in phase one need to continue with ingredients added in this phase as part of your regular lifestyle. These would be:

1. **Coffee/tea.** I can see many of you jumping with joy at this. At this stage, your body and mind are ready to tolerate caffeine and enjoy it occasionally. However, caffeine can become a part of your routine only twice a week if you want to continue to stay detoxed. You can stock up on your favourite coffee/tea but you will need to have it black or with a plant based milk and you will need to have it only twice a week. The benefits of caffeine twice a week will now be a luxury because you will not need the caffeine kick. By now you would be so fresh and full of high energy that the addition of caffeine to the menu may no longer be effective. So while this is added back, it is optional for you to incorporate it.
2. **Tofu/soya paneer.** This plant-based paneer is high in protein and minerals, providing the right muscle power to reduce fatigue. At this stage, addition of proteins is necessary and any soya product which is natural can be added no more than three times a week. Soya, consumed in balanced quantities, is extremely beneficial in pacifying hormones and reducing the risk of cancer. However, having this in larger quantities or daily can interfere with our hormones. Do not have soya nuggets or chunks as those are processed.
3. **Organic eggs.** These serve as the perfect source of animal protein. The white has vitamin D and calcium and the yolk has loads of anti-cancer nutrients such as glutathione, selenium, folate and good fat. This makes organic eggs perfect in balancing your energy levels. I know so many

people who go on detoxification programmes and start feeling fatigued. I am sure that my programme is not going to make you feel fatigued because it is not a normal detoxification programme. By phase three, when you are incorporating a healthy lifestyle to continue to detox, addition of organic eggs ensures that you do not face chronic fatigue because this is a good protein for everyone to have. If you are vegetarian, you can incorporate the next option.

4. **Almond milk.** This plant-based vegan milk is high in protein. As you have understood by now, I am not in favour of milk and milk products in the quantities that they are consumed by adults across the world. Almond milk becomes a yummy substitute then. You can have it at breakfast or put two tablespoons of it in your coffee to get a nutty, delicious flavour.

5. **Small quantities of milk products.** While I am not in favour of milk and milk products in the quantities that the world is using, specifically India, small quantities of these are beneficial for us. You can choose from yoghurt, paneer or ghee. All three have wonderful probiotics which will continue to help our gut and the protein in them will help us stay fresh. Yoghurt and paneer are also richer in calcium than milk, so small quantities of these are beneficial for the bones. However, be very mindful of quantities. As per the recipes listed and the meal plan, when you are leading a restored life, you have to ensure that no more than five per cent of your entire food contains any of these milk products. Use them as a garnishing, dressing or a tiny treat!

6. **Small quantities of sour items.** Amlarasa (sour taste) is one of the main organoleptic entities in foods of present

day, which always tempts the consumer to take it now and then.[25] According to classical Ayurvedic texts, balanced intake of amlarasa in diet helps to maintain functional health, but excessive intake produces signs and symptoms such as teeth hypersensitivity, inflammation of the mucous membrane of the mouth (stomatitis), bad breath (halitosis), heartburn, skin rashes (urticaria), pimples, acne, joint inflammation and joint pain. Use sour items as garnishing in life. Having more quantities of lemon or lime is not going to help you lose weight. If you follow the detox programme as listed, you would in any case lose copious amounts of weight and loads of inches. Hence, it is a myth that a lot of lemon is going to make you lose weight. I know that your flavour comes from a dash of lemon, lime, vinegar, tamarind or that tomato chutney you love, and I am completely with you. Please have these but in smaller quantities. I have a wonderful tomato chutney recipe for you later in this book!

Now that you are prepared with all your ingredients, let's take time in helping you repair your gut, release your toxins, reactivate your healing and restore your balance!

PART TWO

Implementing the Four Phases

*When I set out to cleanse myself,
I cleansed my soul.*

Chapter 1

Repair the Gut—the First Seven Days

The digestive system is our core engine for absorption of nutrients and release of toxins.

Most of us experience acidity, bloating, constipation, mood swings, headaches, sluggishness and/or lack of freshness at some point in our lives. All these are signs of toxins in your gut. However, to accelerate the release of toxins, we first need to calm the gut and repair it so that it can become efficient. The gut is just another name for our digestive or gastrointestinal system. Also referred to as the gastrointestinal tract or digestive tract, our gut is actually a group of organs including the mouth, oesophagus, stomach, pancreas, liver, gall bladder, small intestine, colon and rectum. Most of the process of absorption of nutrients and expelling of toxins happens through the digestive tract. Without an efficient digestive system or gut, the detoxification process cannot be complete and release of toxins is not efficient. A compromised digestive system which does not release toxins absorbs a lower quantity of nutrients, making the immune system weak.

Very often when the gut is compromised, apart from the symptoms of acidity, bloating, constipation, a lot of people, especially women, experience pigmentation, acne and hair fall. My shuddha programme ensures that we repair the gut and all these issues start disappearing. Repairing the gut hence becomes the first step in this sequential ladder of detoxification. Since you already have prepared everything as listed in the previous part of this book, let us deep dive into this phase of your life. This phase is for seven days.

SCHEDULE FOR SEVEN DAYS

Wake up by or before 7.00 a.m.

It is important to not sleep late during phase one of the detoxification. Even if you are sleeping late and getting up late due to the lockdown or your work, at this time, it is important that you wake up before 7.00 a.m. to start revving up your digestive system. A large part of the sluggishness of the digestive system will start disappearing when you do this.

On waking up

Take one tablespoon fresh aloe vera gel (recipe in recipes section) dissolved in water, along with 10 almonds (raw). Do not soak the almonds.

Go to the washroom. Brush your teeth with upward and downward movement and not horizontal movement and ensure that you have a tongue cleaner for cleansing your tongue at the end of the brushing ritual. This is particularly important as the bacteria and fungus can stay stuck on our tongue despite brushing our teeth. Investing in a metal tongue cleaner with blunt sides is the best option. In fact, research has proven that bacteria can form colonies on the tongue, and push aside nutrients required for absorption.[1] This makes it a toxin that erodes your gut microbe. Your gut microbe begins in the mouth and eliminating these bacterial colonies makes space for nutrients to come in to repair your gut microbe.

After coming out of the bathroom, do the following:

Morning ritual

1. Stretch your arms above your head and try and touch the top of your door. Stay like that for 20 seconds. Release.
2. Rotate your shoulders five times towards the back and five times towards the front, then release.
3. Walk at a moderate pace for 10 minutes around the house.
4. Stop and drink 100 millilitres of room temperature water.
5. Repeat the above steps again.

Sit down in a comfortable position, with your spine straight. You can support your spine with pillows or cushions but you should not be slouching. Keep your legs straight and do not sit in a meditative pose if your knees get stiff. You can keep your knees straight in front of you on the bed or you can put a stool in front of you. Then you need to start the gentle breathing exercise of *anulom vilom* or alternate nose breathing as per the below instructions:

1. Always begin from the left nostril. Close the right nostril with your right thumb and inhale slowly to fill up your lungs. The inhalation should not be forceful; it should be gentle and deep. Now, exhale slowly from the right nostril. Similarly, with exhalation, it should be gentle, unhurried and flowing.
2. Inhale back from the right nostril in the same gentle manner, hold for two seconds and exhale deeply and

evenly from the left nostril. If you are a heart patient, do not hold for two seconds; for everybody else, this is beneficial.
3. Inhale again from the left and hold for two seconds and exhale from the right.
4. Repeat this cycle for five minutes, slowly and deeply, without hurrying. Remember: hurry is your enemy.
5. With each inhalation you take, imagine the healing oxygen and white light going into your entire body. With each exhalation that you throw out, visualize a dark grey smoke coming out when you exhale—these are the toxins you are releasing. Continue this visualization for five minutes.
6. After five minutes, take a couple of sips of water.
7. If your arm gets tired, prop it with pillows to support the arm. You can also change your hand as long as you continue this rhythmic flow of inhalation and exhalation.
8. On the first day, only do five minutes. Build up two minutes every day until you get to 15 minutes. And then do 15 minutes every single day.

After pranayama

During the detox period, it is important to nourish ourselves at regular intervals but with smaller and easy to digest quantities of food. The digestive tract needs space and time to start the repair work. When we eat frequent meals, it does not get the space and time. When we overeat, it fills the stomach so much that there is no space for the digestive juices to absorb the nutrients and digest the food efficiently. Hence, the meal plan listed is going to ensure structure and regularity. If you have been skipping breakfast, this is the time to break that habit. We are not looking at any fad diets here so if you have been doing any of the fad diets and have still not felt great, it is time to try cleansing yourself with my shuddha programme completely, so your gut can repair itself.

Just like we need food for nourishment, we also need water at regular intervals. The best thumb rule is to never combine water with food. This interferes with the digestive process. Also, unlike with most other detox programmes, I will not recommend drinking large quantities of water in one sitting. This dilutes the nutrients and puts load on the kidneys. Always space your water out—the thumb rule is to have one glass of water every 90 minutes of waking time. You can have water 30 minutes before any meal, but you need to wait for one hour after you have eaten to drink water or any other kind of liquid, including herbal and green teas.

9.00 a.m., Breakfast:

Prepare six tablespoons of poha (recipe in the recipes section) with one tablespoon extra virgin olive oil. It is important to adhere to this time and have this particular breakfast to begin the day by pacifying the gut. The preparation of poha is extremely light and easy to digest. Having this daily ensures that your energy is high first thing in the morning. For people who eat a late or heavy breakfast or even skip breakfast, this will be a big change because they would have been habituated to another schedule. Shifting to a light breakfast like this ensures a calming energy going to the digestive tract first thing in the morning. Combined with the extra virgin olive oil which enhances the healing of the gut, this light Indian breakfast keeps us mentally alert. The spices mentioned in the recipe also cleanse our gut and are anti-inflammatory. For those of you who are not familiar with the taste of extra virgin olive oil are going to find it either bitter or burning in your throat. This is natural, do not worry. Over time, you will get habituated to the taste.

10.00 a.m.: Have 250 millilitres of room temperature water.

11.00 a.m.: One cup of green tea with coriander and ginger (recipe in recipes section).

1.00 p.m., Lunch: Have six to eight tablespoons of khichdi prepared with one tablespoon of extra virgin olive oil (recipe in recipes section). Eat slowly, and take your time to chew. Do not talk while eating your meal. You can put on soothing music during lunch. There are different recipes for khichdi given for each day, however, the common factor is whatever leafy greens you can find in your local vegetable market. Options of these are listed; please ensure that the khichdi is rotated as per different vegetables listed and different seasoning/tadka listed.

After lunch: Lie down on the left side of your body for 20 minutes with eyes closed. This will enable the digestive system to start digesting the food efficiently. You can put meditative music on in the background to help lull you into slumber. Ideally, if you can sleep at this time, it will help repair the gut faster.

2.00 p.m.: 250 millilitres of room temperature water.

3.00 p.m.: One cup of green tea with mint, home-made spices and honey (recipe in recipes section).

4.00 p.m.: Have 250 millilitres of room temperature water.

5.30 p.m.: One cup or 200 millilitres of vegetable soup (recipe in recipes section). There are seven recipes for soup listed, please have a different one each day.

6.30 p.m., Dinner: Have five tablespoons of varan (an indian dish made of dal), five tablespoons of cooked vegetables, five tablespoons of boiled rice. Once the food is on the plate, drizzle one tablespoon of extra virgin olive oil on the rice. Eat slowly, and take time to chew. Do not talk while eating your meal. You can put on soothing music. Recipes of all these preparations are in the recipes section. It is important to cook as per recipes given for nutrients of all foods and vegetables to be preserved for the purpose of repair and absorption.

9.00 p.m.: Have one glass of water and take a 20-minute moderate-paced walk.

9:30 p.m.: Have one cup of chamomile tea with one tablespoon organic honey.

10.00 p.m.: Please get into bed with a book or music. List of recommended reading and music at bedtime is listed in the next part. It is important to get into bed at 10.00 p.m. every day even if you are not habituated to sleeping at that time. Once you get into bed and do calming activities like reading or listening to soothing music, over a few weeks, sleep will automatically start enveloping you around this time. Going to sleep between 10.00 and 11.00 p.m. ensures that you get eight hours of sleep. Sleep is one of our pillars in repairing our gut to release toxins and hence, not sleeping at this time or not sleeping for eight hours compromises your detoxification journey.

What can you expect in seven days?

When we change any habit or even a house, we experience some kind of resistance and withdrawal from our mind and body. This is natural. Similarly, you are not used to eating or living like this, you will experience a period of discomfort.

Just like when you shift to a new, beautiful home, you do not sleep well for a couple of weeks; the boxes are lying around and sunlight doesn't fall in the direction you are used to on your bed and so on. But you do not run away from your beautiful home, you make it comfortable. In the same manner, our digestive system, body and mind are very adaptable and flexible. With consistent input, they start adapting to the new structure. This new therapeutic structure will help you in the detoxification process and get you started on your healing journey.

Below is the list of symptoms you will experience if the number of toxins in your body are too many:

1. **Weight loss.** For those of you who have been eating frequent meals, eating higher quantities or eating differently, and not adding any unsaturated fat to your meals, you can expect a couple of kilos of weight loss. This is because inflammation levels are reducing and the gut is prepared to release toxins. For someone who does not need to lose weight, this can be disturbing. However, the body balances itself out and for those who need to gain weight, you'll gain it back later. However, for someone who needs to lose weight, the weight loss will continue even in the next two phases.
2. **Bloating, acidity or constipation**. If the gut is ravaged to a large extent, these symptoms are natural. When you experience more bloating or acidity than you can bear, you can have chamomile tea with crushed ginger and organic honey to pacify your gut.
3. **Headaches.** Unlike what medical science believes, headaches are a symptom of something going wrong in your gut. If you are experiencing bloating, acidity or constipation, headaches will be common. Sometimes

headaches also come because of lack of hydration and constipation. Our brain cells get dehydrated first, before our body cells, hence headaches are a sign that you are not having enough water. As explained in the previous part, one glass of water every 90 minutes of waking time gets rid of constipation and headaches.

4. **Lethargy.** It is extremely common in the initial stages of purification of the mind and body. This is because all the energy of the body is directed towards the digestive system to repair it. Then, the rest of the organs and body do not get enough energy and you start feeling sluggish, slow and sleepy. This is truly a good sign and you must listen to your body at this stage. If you are feeling sluggish and lethargic, just lie down and go to sleep without worrying about what time of the day or night it is. The more energy you give to your digestive system by reducing energy dissipation for other activities, the faster your toxins will get released.

5. **Boredom.** This is common when you have to eat milder and different food from what you have been used to. The food items that are mentioned in this programme are simple and do not have the dramatic flavours that you are used to. So you will feel like you are eating the same thing every day, but this is not true. In the recipes section, there are different recipes given for each day of the week, even for the first phase. The vegetables are different, the tempering is different and the soups are different. As you get used to these mild and mellow flavours, you will begin to enjoy the simplicity of these meals over stronger salt or spice-flavoured foods you have been used to.

6. **Hunger.** Feeling hungry is natural because you are used to eating frequent meals or meals that make you

feel fuller. The entire purpose of the detoxification is to give space to the digestive juices and reactivate your gut healing. Eating larger quantities of food is detrimental to this process. Hunger is a good sign because this means that your stomach is getting the right amount of space to start repairing your digestive tract. For those of you who have been overeating and need to lose weight, please remember: the stomach is a plastic bag. It expands with more food. When you start eating lesser quantities, it takes time to shrink back to its original size and in the weeks that it is taking to shrink back, there is an empty space which will give you the illusion of hunger. Also, often we are actually thirsty when we feel hungry. Always have a glass of water if you feel hungry. Over a few days, you will realize that you are not as hungry as it is your body needing to hydrate itself.

Chapter 2

Release the Toxins—in Three Weeks

If you have reached here successfully by doing everything specified in phase one, you would have started feeling the first effects of the detoxification process. You would have lost a little bit of weight and the lethargy would have started settling down. If you are still facing bloating, acidity, constipation, headaches or extreme lethargy, you need to continue the seven-day cleanse phase for seven more days. Continued symptoms like these are indicative of higher level of toxins in the body. However, most people start feeling lighter by day five. Now you are ready to add variety and agility to your next phase of detoxification.

PHASE TWO SCHEDULE

Wake Up by 7.00 a.m.

If you have been getting into bed by 10.00 p.m., by now you would have started getting into a semi-habit. It will still take you three more weeks for this habit to stabilize. Please make sure that you do not break this habit during this detoxification period. The key to your digestive system repairing is to get it revved up first thing in the morning.

On waking up

Take one tablespoon of fresh aloe vera gel (mandatory) dissolved in water, along with 10 almonds (raw). Do not soak the almonds.

Go to the washroom. Brush your teeth in the manner explained in phase one and ensure you clean your tongue. Now that your detoxification journey is going to be accelerated, this cleansing ritual is more important. After brushing your teeth, if you have bath, please ensure that after the bath you use the towel to scrub your entire body while you dry it. This will rev up your circulation. It is preferred that you finish having your bath at this time.

Morning ritual (different from phase one):

1. Stretch your arms above your head and try and touch the top of your door. Stay like that for 20 seconds. Release.
2. Rotate your shoulders five times towards the back and five times towards the front, then release.
3. Touch your toes and hold for 20 seconds.
4. Put your feet apart and do 20 alternate toe touches, very slowly. Do not use jerky moments as that can injure your back.
5. Walk at a moderate pace for 20 minutes around the house, barefoot.
6. Drink 200 millilitres of room temperature water after you're done walking.

Do these two breathing exercises mentioned below:

Sit down in a comfortable position, with your spine straight. Support your spine with pillows or cushions but do not slouch. Keep your legs straight, do not sit in a meditative pose if your knees get stiff. By now, if your knees or joints did get stiff, some of the stiffness would have started reducing. But you can keep your knees straight in front of you on the bed or you can put a stool in front of you.

1. Anulom vilom or alternate nose breathing: 15 minutes
This is already explained in phase one. You need to do this for 15 minutes without a break. If you get tired in between, you can sip water and continue. Do not forget that your first inhalation has to be from the left and your last exhalation should also be from the left. Read the instructions mentioned under phase one again if you have forgotten the process.

2. Brahmri or humming bee: five minutes
Close your mouth and keep your teeth slightly apart. Bring the tip of your tongue to the space behind the front teeth. Maintain this position of the mouth throughout the practice, frequently checking to ensure that the jaw remains relaxed. Close each ear with your thumbs, place index fingers at midpoint of the forehead—just above the eyebrows—reach the middle, ring and pinkie fingers across the eyes so that the tips of these fingers press gently against the bridge of the nose.

Now take a long, deep breath in through the nostrils, bringing the breath all the way into the belly. Begin to exhale slowly, making a steady, low-pitched 'om' sound at the back of the throat—like the humming of a bee. Focus on making the sound soft, smooth and steady. The positioning of the tongue encourages the vibration to resonate throughout your brain, cleansing and rejuvenating it. Keep your awareness to the centre of your head. You need to let the sound fill up your brain and feel the vibrations on the sides of your face. Begin with five long repetitions. Slowly build this up to 10, and as you practise daily, you will realize that each repetition or exhalation of breath will become longer. Ideally, each repetition should be one-minute long and this can be achieved after a month of daily practise.

The practice of Brahmri cleanses your brain and helps your thyroid and endocrine system become efficient. These exercises need to be done in the order listed above. This is required to start reducing toxin levels almost immediately along with repairing your gut. To get these results, consistency and regularity is a must.

After pranayama

In phase two, your stomach is ready for a little bit of raw cleansing. Hence, phase two nutrition is different from phase one where we were preparing your gut to be able to start digesting raw foods. Many of you may face discomfort with raw foods in the second phase, if that is the case, please extend phase one by another week. Also remember that it is extremely important to nourish ourselves at regular intervals in the combinations and timings listed in order to expel toxins in this phase. If you were skipping breakfast before starting out with my programme, by now, you would begin to feel hungry in the morning on some days. Even if you don't, you still need to follow the timings so that your new habits can be formed through the consistency of input. The shuddha programme works wonders when consistent input is followed to release toxins.

The thumb rule for water continues in this phase as well—instead of large quantities of water, you need to have water consistently throughout the day so that toxins from all parts of the body can be pulled and flushed out through your colon. Remember to never combine water with food. Have one glass of water every 90 minutes of waking time. You can have water

30 minutes before any meal, but you need to wait for one hour after you have eaten any meal to drink water or any other kind of liquid, including herbal and green teas.

9.00 a.m., Breakfast: Have a bowl of room temperature fruit of any of the available fruits from the list below, combined with 10 almonds and 10 pistachios.

1. Apple
2. Papaya
3. Pomegranate
4. Red grapes
5. Green grapes
6. Black grapes
7. Muskmelon
8. Jamun
9. Pears
10. Pineapple

Note: Do not exceed more than three fruits, rotate fruits if there are many available in the market instead of eating only one or two kinds of fruits every day. The entire fruit bowl should be medium-sized. Just because it is fruit does not mean you can overeat it. Balance in food quantities, no matter how healthy the foods are, is important to aid the detoxification process.

10.00 a.m.: Have 250 millilitres of room temperature water.

11.00 a.m.: Have one cup green tea with coriander and ginger.

1.00 p.m., Lunch:

Meal one: Two methi rotis, one bowl curry vegetable, one bowl cut salad

Meal two: 10 tablespoons vegetable pulao, coriander curry, one bowl cut salad
Meal three: Two brown rice-quinoa rotis, one bowl curry vegetable, one bowl cut salad
Meal four: Oats upma with vegetables, one bowl cut salad

Rotate the above options and have option one on the fifth day again. Do not have the same option every day. Different salad options are listed for different days—please rotate.

After lunch: Lie down on the left side of your body for 20 minutes with your eyes closed. This is vital for the digestive system to begin digesting the food efficiently. Put meditative music in the background to help you into slumber.

2.00 p.m.: Have 250 millilitres of room temperature water.

3.00 p.m.: One cup green tea with mint, home-made spices and honey (recipe in recipes section).

4.00 p.m.: Have 250 millilitres of popsicle water (recipe in recipes section).

5.00 p.m.: Walk in the office or around the home for 10 minutes. Stretch your arms above your head and touch the top of the door and stay for 30 seconds. Then touch your toes and stay for 30 seconds. If you cannot touch your toes, go down till whatever level is comfortable. Then keep your feet two ft. apart and do 20 alternate toe touches. This is crucial to rev up your circulation.

5.30 p.m.: Have tulsi green tea with any one of the options for snacks below (rotate options):
Snack one: 12–15 roasted makhanas
Snack two: Five tablespoons murmura bhel
Snack three: Five tablespoons chivda

6.30 p.m., Dinner:
Meal one: One serving of brown rice salad with vegetables
Meal two: Five tablespoons of quinoa pulao with one bowl of cut salad
Meal three: One palak roti, one bowl of curry vegetable and one bowl of cut salad
Meal four: Moong dal broth and one bowl of cut salad

Rotate the above options and have option one on the fifth day again. Do not have the same option every day.

Eat slowly, and take time to chew. Do not talk while eating your meal. You can put on soothing music. All the recipes are available in the recipe section. It is important to cook as per the given recipes for nutrients of all foods and vegetables to be preserved to achieve maximum levels of repair and absorption.

9.00 p.m.: Have one glass of water and do 20 minutes of moderate-paced walk.

9:30 p.m.: Have one cup of chamomile tea with one tablespoon organic honey added.

10.00 p.m.: Please get into bed with a book or music. List of recommended reading and music at bedtime is listed in the next part.

By now, the habit of getting into bed by 10.00 p.m. would have started to develop. Many people on my shuddha programme start enjoying this by this point in the process. It is important to get into bed at 10.00 p.m. every day even if you are not habituated to sleeping at that time. Once you get into bed and do calming activities like reading or listening to soothing music, over a few weeks, you will start to naturally feel sleepy at the same time everyday.

SIDE EFFECTS OF THIS PHASE YOU NEED TO BE PREPARED FOR

You may face skin itching. If you have many toxins, the digestive system can get overwhelmed and not be able to expel them all through bowel movements. In this scenario, you can face itchiness or redness. The ritual of scrubbing your body with a towel after a bath, as given in the morning schedule, will bring down this itching. Drinking more water will also bring it down. Apply aloe vera gel on the irritated skin to calm it down.

You may go to the washroom frequently. You can expect three to four bowel movements and expect to urinate frequently. This is extremely normal as now the toxins are coming out. Many people are not used to more than one bowel movement and may end up feeling weak. Do not worry; you will soon get used to it and it is better to expel the toxins than to carry them around in your colon. Therefore, welcome the three bowel movements a day as part of your daily life if you want to remain shuddha and detoxed.

You can feel constipated. Sometimes our water intake is enough but our digestive system is weak and is unable to flush out so much soluble fibre from vegetables, especially if you have not been used to having so many vegetables and salads. The extra virgin olive oil written in the quantities in the recipes has to be had in these specified quantities to ensure that there is easy passage of food from the colon to the rectal area for excretion. This oil lubrication is imperative for the detoxification process, so do not reduce your extra virgin olive oil quantitiy; you can increase it if you face constipation. Also, start taking insoluble fibre in the form of psyllium husk (isabgol)—two tablespoons dissolved in 200 millilitres of water—along with one tablespoon extra virgin olive oil, followed by another 200 millilitres of water. The best time to take this would be after your evening exercise. This will ensure that the constipation disappears.

You will lose weight. For those of you who need to lose weight, in this phase you will end up losing three kilograms or more. This is healthy as the toxins and the bad fat are getting released. Till we do not release the bad fat, we won't be able to build a strong immune system that can build good muscle.

You will sleep better. The regularity of eating on time and eating foods that are repairing your gut will ensure better sleep. This will start happening only after the second week of the second phase. This is a good sign because good sleep ensures that the digestive system is getting strong enough to expel the toxins. Sleep also repairs and rejuvenates us and if you have had any health issues like type two diabetes and/or hypertension, they will start to come under control. Watch out for low sugar or low blood pressure if you have any of the above conditions, you may need to get your dosages altered and reduced by your doctor as your body is healing and dependency on drugs will start reducing as toxin load reduces.

You will start to see clearer skin. For those of you who have had acne issues, after the second week of the second phase, acne breakouts will start to reduce if your constipation has disappeared. This is because your gut bacteria and microbe are changing. Acne is the result of bad bacteria and hormonal imbalance. When you start to follow a detoxification programme and your colon cleanse is happening naturally, the acne spots will reduce and the scars that remain will start healing faster.

Chapter 3

Reactivate Your Rhythm—in Four Weeks

Welcome to the third and most important phase! If you have made it till here, you first need to applaud yourself. Reaching the third phase is not easy; your commitment to self-care and personal well-being is now very high. You have also started experiencing some tiny miracles within yourself. These will be:

You are calmer. Eating less, on time and the right kind of combinations along with doing the breath work and the morning ritual helps us calm the agitation in our brain. Simply put, the same things that used to irritate you are now not so bad. Your tolerance levels would have gone up and people around you would have started to notice this.

Your skin is healthier. Our skin is our largest organ and eating healthy, having a cleansed gut and an efficient liver means pigmentation and acne starts reducing and natural oils from the oils you have been taking in the last two phases have started to make your skin feel hydrated and younger.

You have lost weight. Release of toxins often comes with weight loss. Fluctuating hormones are due to the toxins inside us and when people get onto my shuddha programme, their hormones start getting pacified. Fluctuating hormones block weight loss and now this impediment has also been removed, leading to weight loss in women who usually don't lose weight through extreme diet programmes. For men, a reduction in belly fat means that you have reduced your risk of heart disease. All due to making your mind and body shuddha!

You excrete stool twice a day, at least. When the gut is repaired and toxins are released on a daily basis, it means you go to the bathroom more than once. A lot of people who come to me and say that they are not constipated because they go only once, do not realize how many toxins are in their body and colon. By the time you reach phase three, gut repair has started so it now efficiently releases toxins on a daily basis. If you are not excreting stool, a minimum of twice a day, it means your water intake or the consumption of extra virgin olive oil is less than what I have prescribed in phase one and two. Please be very mindful, even if you think that the quantities are too much or too little, as per my shuddha programme, these are the quantities you need to release the toxins.

Now that your liver is efficient and your digestive system is beginning to look squeaky clean, what can we expect in phase three?

What we did in phase one and two was to get you used to a structure and help you release toxins. However, the continued release of toxins over a period of time is what provides the foundation for a healthy immune system. A lot of people go on a detox and then go back to eating normally, even though their normal is what caused the toxins in the first place. When we repair the digestive system and release toxins, we also have to stabilize this process. Stability cannot come without consistency. And hence, this phase is all about following the rhythm every day, day after day.

In this phase, we also have to add protein. Proteins take

longer to digest but are required for a healthy immune system, muscle mass and freshness levels. Lack of protein causes fatigue. If you could ask your genes what kinds of foods are best for your health, they would have a simple answer: one-third protein, one-third fat and one-third carbohydrates. A diet with 65 per cent carbohydrates, which often is what normal people eat in some meals, causes our genes to work overtime to cause inflammation in the body, and risk of cardiovascular disease, some cancers, dementia and type two diabetes.[2]

It was important for us to have a lighter and easy to digest programme for you in phases one and two because any burden of heavy digestive activity would have hindered the process of releasing your toxins. That is the reason most proteins were eliminated from phases one and two. Now that your digestive system is repaired and we need to continue the rhythm of healing, we need to help your body adapt to the best balance in order to stay detoxed for life.

With the addition of proteins, your schedule will be slightly different.

On waking up

Take one tablespoon fresh aloe vera gel (mandatory) dissolved in water, along with 10 almonds (raw). Do not soak the almonds. This ritual continues and, ideally, should continue through the larger phase of your life. At a later stage, you could reduce the frequency of this to four to five days in a week. In this phase, aloe vera gel will continue to repair your gut and stabilize it so that your toxin load is uninterruptedly getting released on a daily basis and the gut is now ready to absorb nutrients from food at a much higher capacity.

Go to the washroom. Brush your teeth as explained in phase one and ensure you clean your tongue. Have a bath, and after the bath use your towel to scrub your entire body as you dry it to rev up your circulation. This is especially important for those who want to continue losing more weight or those who still have skin eruptions, pigmentation or acne.

After coming out of the bathroom, do the following:

Morning ritual (different from phases one and two)

1. **Do wrist rotations.** Hold your arms in front of you and rotate your wrist with your palms closed into a fist—10 times clockwise and 10 times anticlockwise very slowly.
2. **Do shoulder rotations.** Rotate your shoulders 10 times towards the back and 10 times towards the front, then release. Relax.
3. **Do neck rotations.** Very slowly, starting at the front, drop your chin to your chest and rotate it very slowly to the left side and back and right side of your head and then bring it back to your chest and drop your chin to your chest. Repeat this three times on the left side and three times on the right side.
4. **Spine stretch.** Stretch your arms above your head and try and touch the top of your door. Stay like that for 30 seconds. Release.
5. **Toe touch.** Touch your toes and hold for 30 seconds.
6. **Alternate toe touches.** Put your feet apart, and do 20 alternate toe touches, very slowly. Do not use jerky moments as that can injure your back.
7. **Walking.** Walk at a moderate pace for 30 minutes around the house. Do it barefoot.
8. **Water intake.** Drink 200 millilitres of room temperature water after you finish the walk.

Why is it important to continue all of the above?

Why can't you just get up and go for a walk? This is because when we wake up, our circulation levels are erratic and the rotations we do help us increase circulation and reduce stiffness levels. The stretches and the toe touches open up our spine and help it become supple. A supple spine while walking ensures a better posture and a healthier walking routine. And if you are someone who has been used to not exercising or over exercising, the entire stretching schedule before your walk is going to reduce muscle soreness or injury. Always remember, whether it is nutrition, exercise or life, warming up will always help us be prepared and increase efficiency.

Continue breathing exercises

Both the breathing exercises have multiple benefits. While alternate nose breathing continuously repairs your digestive system starting from the oesophagus down to your rectal area, the humming bee helps bring freshness and memory. When we are looking at a shuddha you, your mind and body should be in a higher state of consciousness so that it can expel all of the existing toxins around you. The toxins around you through the air, water, chemicals and pesticides are not going to disappear. My programme is helping you repair your mind and body to such a level that they get automatically rejected and expelled from your body very efficiently. And these two breathing exercises play an extremely important role in expelling these toxins.

After pranayama

In phase three, you are ready for protein! Hence, the phase three nutrition expands to add variety and taste in your choices and the protein enhances your energy and freshness levels. Since you are introducing proteins after a long gap, you can expect a little bit of heaviness when you eat any of the protein meals listed below. This is normal and your stomach will soon adapt to it. Remember to adhere to the prescribed quantities, otherwise the purpose of the detox is not going to be complete. As much as 20 per cent of your plate always has to be empty, just like your stomach. Only then can the digestive juices work towards absorbing nutrients and expelling toxins efficiently. By now, the rhythm of your hunger has been set. If you've never had breakfast, you definitely get hungry at this time because during phases one and two, you ate at this time. The reason that phase three sets the rhythm is this: the habits that you inculcate in phases one and two need to get cemented. If you slip up on those, your detoxification is not going to be complete. Reinforcing this rhythm is the purpose of phase three.

The thumb rules for water continue in this phase too—instead of large quantities of water, you need to have consistent water throughout the day so that toxins from all parts of the body can be pulled and flushed out through your colon. Remember to never combine water with food. You can have water 30 minutes before any meal, but you need to wait for one hour after you have eaten any meal to drink water or any other kind of liquid, including herbal and green teas.

9.00 a.m., Breakfast:

1. Quinoa upma, one medium-sized bowl
2. Oats upma, one medium-sized bowl
3. Oats porridge, one medium-sized bowl
4. Moong dal omelette (one only), have with one tablespoon mint chutney

Rotate the above options and have option one on the fifth day again. Each of these options has higher protein than your previous options. They are also high in fibre, making the process of detoxification continuous and proficient.

10.00 a.m.: Have 250 millilitres of room temperature water.

11.00 a.m.: Have one cup of green tea with coriander and ginger.

12.30 p.m.: Have one glass water and one bowl of cut salad. You can choose from any of the cut salad recipes, however, have a different one each day. Rotate.

1.00 p.m., Lunch:

1. Hundred grams of tofu bhurji, one methi/coriander roti and one bowl of curry vegetable
2. One bowl moong dal varan, one brown rice-quinoa roti and one dry vegetable preparation
3. Two full boiled eggs and one cup soup. You can choose from any of the soup recipes, however, have a different one each day. Rotate. If you are a vegetarian, you can replace boiled eggs with one medium-sized bowl of quinoa pulao.

Rotate the above options and have the first option on the fourth day again. Do not have the same option every day.

After lunch: Lie down on the left side of your body for 20 minutes with your eyes closed. This habit should be continued throughout your life as it will help you develop a strong digestive system, which is the foundation for releasing toxins efficiently.

The importance of afternoon naps:

By now you would have got into the habit of taking a small nap in the afternoon as part of your rhythm. In this phase, this rhythm needs to be set to a habit in such a way that you feel sleepy at the same time after lunch every day. This will help your digestive system stay strong and make the toxin release process easier. Afternoon naps, or siestas, are practised in many Mediterranean and Latin American countries such as Spain and Argentina as well as Japan. Called *inemuri* in Japanese, a mishmash of the verb for being present as well as one for sleeping, or *hirune* which means nap, it is a habit practised by most office goers. Simply put, it means 'nodding off.' Many Japanese companies have provided daybeds to employees in order to get them to have a 20-minute nap post lunch. Brigitte Steger, a University of Cambridge lecturer who has studied Japanese sleeping habits, distinguishes between a *hirune* and *inemuri*.

'Inemuri is very different from a nap,' says Dr Steger. 'It's not taking off your shoes and withdrawing, it's actually, "I am actually at work." You are still officially working even if you drop off.'[3] And researchers in United Kingdom have found that the time just before you fall asleep in this afternoon nap time is when the most beneficial cardiovascular changes take place. With science supporting an afternoon nap and ancient yoga and Ayurveda already promoting it, there is no reason that you should not adapt to this practice, especially if you want a healthy heart. Short afternoon naps post lunch have also demonstrated a reduce in high blood pressure and inflammation levels.[4] When you incorporate these into your daily life, all the excuses of 'I am at work' start disappearing as everybody can spare 20 minutes after lunch with their phone on silent. So continue this habit and make sure you have a comfortable chair or sofa in your office. Some of my patients ensure that they go to their car and nod off for 20 minutes when there is no free couch available in the office! This health-first practice has helped them reverse type two diabetes and hypertension. The link between detoxification and an afternoon nap is very strong: a higher than normal BP means that we have stress in the body and stress is a toxin. An afternoon nap reduces levels of stress, thereby also expelling other toxins like excess sugar and cholesterol deposits in the body and heart.

2.00 p.m.: Have 250 millilitres of room temperature water.

3.00 p.m.: Have one cup of green tea made with mint, homemade spices and honey (recipe in recipes section).

4.00 p.m.: Have 250 millilitres of popsicle water (recipe in recipes section).

5.00 p.m.: Walk in the office or around the home for 15 minutes. Stretch your arms above your head and touch the top of the door and stay for 30 seconds. Remember, your arms rarely go above your head—they are engaged with a phone or laptop, or cooking and doing tasks. Putting your arms above your head a few times a day is going to release the stress trapped in your back and shoulders. After this, touch your toes and stay for 30 seconds. If you cannot touch your toes, bend down till whatever is comfortable. Then keep your feet two ft. apart and do 20 alternate toe touches. This is important to rev up your circulation in order for the toxins to get released. Follow up with 250 millilitres of water.

5.30 p.m.: Eat one bowl of any three fruits, choose from the options given in phase two. Combine this with 10 pistachios and one cup of tulsi green tea. It is important to have fruits as snacks separately from meals. This ensures that the sugar in fruit does not get combined with the sugar (carbohydrates convert to sugar in the body) in your main meal and cause a sugar rush. The antioxidants and fibre in fruits are protective and need to be absorbed in isolation by the gut. Combining fruits with nuts ensures that the sugar in fruits does not spike as nuts reduce it immediately. Nuts are a wonderful source of good fats and proteins which are again important for helping you stay fresh and keep a calm mind.

6.30 p.m., Dinner:
Meal one: One serving of brown rice salad with vegetables
Meal two: Five tablespoons of quinoa pulao with one bowl of cut salad
Meal three: One palak roti, one bowl of curry vegetable and one bowl of cut salad
Meal four: Moong dal soup with one bowl of cut salad

Recipes for the above meal options are available in the recipe section of this book. Rotate the above options and have option one on the fifth day again. Do not have the same option every day.

Eat slowly, and take time to chew. Do not talk during your meal. You can put on soothing music during lunch. It is important to cook as per the given recipes for nutrients of all foods and vegetables are preserved to ensure repair and absorption.

9.00 p.m.: Have one glass of water and do 20 minutes of a moderate-paced walk. It is important to have a two hour gap between the walk and the dinner. And this can only happen when you finish your dinner by 7.00 p.m. Slow to moderate paced walks two hours after dinner have been shown to improve the quality of sleep. Do not exercise more than this as it can disrupt sleep. Do not walk fast as that can be detrimental to the heart at night.

9.30 p.m.: Have one cup of chamomile tea with one tablespoon of organic honey.

10.00 p.m.: Please get into bed with a book or music. Recommended reading and music for bedtime is listed in the next part.

WHAT THIS PHASE ENSURES

When you follow the above mentioned plan, you are creating a stable foundation for the detoxification process to be natural, rhythmic and continuous. What you are doing above is recaptured in these very few simple steps below.

1. **Consistency.** Whatever you have adapted to in phases one, two and three in terms of timings, pranayama and stretching, it has to be done consistently to lead a life which is high on energy and low on toxins. Toxins are everywhere, and these daily habits will release them on a day-to-day basis.
2. **The rhythm develops into a habit.** Now that you have come this far, you need to make this shuddha life your new normal. Your old normal did not work for you and hence you needed the detox. Incorporating a detox life into your new normal is part of setting a rhythm for a new and healthy life.
3. **Helps you understand what you are eating.** When we are reactivating and setting our rhythm, we need to understand what your food groups consist of and what you can choose in order to remain squeaky clean. Every carbohydrate is not created equal, every protein is not

created equal and every fat is not created equal. In the next few pages, we will understand this and recognize how to make swaps so that you are able to reach for the best foods that help you stay healthy.

4. **Helps you realize the importance of quantities and timings.** Yes, you have adapted to the timings as per phases one and two, however, in phase three, you will feel like eating more as a reward. Why? Because you are feeling good and you are feeling leaner and fresher. You feel like you deserve a little bit of cheese, some snacks, a little dessert or a party. And of course you do, for prioritizing your health and not giving in to your cravings during the detox. And that's why small indulgences will be added in the next phase. Our detoxification work is not complete yet. Why? It's because the consistency and rhythm you have developed needs to become a habit. This happens now as we are mindful of our quantities. Your stomach size has already shrunk. The stomach is an elastic bag, if we expand it and eat more, it stays expanded and makes us put on weight, crave carbohydrates and hence collect toxins. As we have shrunk the stomach size in phases one and two, by phase three, your hunger signals are different. Since your brain is calmer, you are more in touch with your body to be able to recognize the difference between hunger for food and hunger for water. If by now you are not recognizing the signals, the next part of my book, which is about understanding your emotions to help you stay detoxed, will also help you get in touch with the signals.

Chapter 4

Restore Your Balance

The human body is a subset of the earth. It is nurtured by akash, vayu, agni, jal, prithvi—space, air, fire, water and earth. In the process of churning and growing, we usually end up focusing on four out of these five. We focus on breath (vayu), proteins and oils (agni), water (jal) and vegetables and fruits (prithvi). But not on the self—the space for self-nurturing (akash)

When we detoxify ourselves, we activate akash. Akash is time/space for self, *I* is on our plates—by eating 20 per cent less than our bodily needs/hunger, we make space for digestive juices to absorb the nutrients and release the toxins, hence healing the digestive tract. We can choose to activate akash via portion control, not eating after sunset and keeping aside 20 minutes post lunch for ourselves. And that is the secret to staying detoxed on a daily basis for the rest of our lives. As you embark on this journey of detoxing yourself with the first three steps implemented, you are now ready to restore your balance by understanding this principle of akash.

The shuddha programme activates akash.

At the heart of a restored mind-body balance is akash. I learnt this little secret in 2008 when I healed my rheumatoid arthritis. Overeating, not giving time to the self for self-nurturing, all of this leads to an increase in toxins and invites diseases. We run from one task to the other and our brain is never empty. If we are sitting quietly, we are unable to enjoy that quiet time without doing something. If we can't find anything else, we pick up our phone and start scrolling on social media. Why? It is because of the restlessness of the brain and the imbalance of hormones in our brain and body. When we detoxify ourselves, these hormones start getting balanced, we start shedding the excess and the feel-good hormones also start to increase. When serotonin and oxytocin increase and cortisol reduces, it leads to reduced fluctuations of the mind.

Serotonin is responsible for your feelings of happiness.[5] It is a neurotransmitter that acts as the body's natural antidepressant and pain reliever. Oxytocin is our love hormone. When we learn to accept ourselves and self-nurture, we also have more love to give to others. Touching, hugs and expressing love and gratitude increase our levels of oxytocin. Cortisol, on the other hand, is our stress hormone which drastically reduces with the detox programme. When we practise akash, these three hormones are balanced with each other—the excess gets released and lower levels increase to maintain the balance we need.

And as we start practising the four Rs, the fourth R is truly about practising akash for our restored balance to stay intact.

In this phase, you can continue with the timings and exercises of the last phase. However, you can add some of the larger list of items like regular consumption of organic eggs and oily fish as your proteins. However, consumption of any animal protein should only be 10 per cent of the entire meal. Since this phase is establishing your new normal, there are certain pillars that ensure the continuity of your new normal for a detoxed life.

Always include vegetables in some form. By including vegetables for lunch and dinner, you ensure the antioxidants and fibre which expel toxins on a regular basis are in abundance. Without vegetables, your risk of producing inflammatory toxins increases. Hence, you must always have them in some form or the other—a cup of soup, one bowl of sabji and a simple cut salad. The presence of all three will ensure that 50 per cent of your meal consists of vegetables.

Be mindful of portion size. We have already discussed that the presence of akash in your digestive system ensures that the digestive juices absorb nutrients and expel toxins much faster. Hence, overeating is a clear way of derailing your detoxed life; always eat a little less than your hunger. How do you know when to stop? If you want to do a calorie count instead of tuning to your body's signs, here is a simple trick: calculate your body mass index (BMI)—there are many BMI calculators available online—and eat 20 per cent less calories of the intake specified for your height. For example, if you are a five-feet-three-inches tall woman weighing 60 kilograms, you should be consuming 1800 calories to maintain your weight. So you need to consume 20 per cent less than 1800 because that will ensure better digestion, faster release of toxins and higher immunity. If you are moderately active, you should not be eating more than 1500 calories. Measuring calories is extremely simple: carbohydrates and proteins are four calories per gram and fat is nine calories per gram. Since your meal is going to consist of these three, it will be easy for you to calculate your meal calories and maintain the 20 per cent reduction. Since all calories are not created equal as I have already explained in my chapter about understanding your foods, a good mix for 1500 calories will be as below:

Table 1

Meal	Time	Description	Calories
Breakfast	9.00 a.m.	One bowl or seven to eight tablespoons of oats/quinoa upma	300
Snack	11.00 a.m.	One green tea, one apple, 10 pistachios	150
Lunch	1.00 p.m.	One roti (choose from the rotis listed in the recipes section) with one small bowl of vegetable, five to six tablespoons cut salad and half a bowl of varan which is about five tablespoons, one tablespoon extra virgin olive oil on salad	350
Snack	3.00 p.m.	Herbal tea with honey with one bowl of papaya, 10 almonds	150
Soup	6.00 p.m.	100 millilitres of any one of the soups listed except pea soup. If it is pea soup, the calorie intake will be higher	150/200

Meal	Time	Description	Calories
Dinner	7.00 p.m.	Five tablespoons of any of the permitted carbohydrates—brown rice, quinoa or white rice—with one bowl vegetable and a bowl of cut salad. You can also have a maximum of eight tablespoons of veg pulao or brown rice or tea as that already consists vegetables, combined with cut salad and 1 tablespoon extra virgin olive oil	350
Dessert	9.00 p.m.	2 dates	50
Total calorie intake/day			1500

Remember, less food will not help you lose weight. Many of you would have looked at the this sample table and said that you actually eat less than this. This may be true but it also means that you have difficulty losing weight, releasing toxins and or have some belly fat. The balance to continuously detox ourselves as well as stay in a healthy weight range is to nourish ourselves continuously till 7.00 p.m. Without doing this, if you skip meals or have longer gaps or eat late, our body goes into fat storage. This is a message from the entire digestive cycle of releasing toxins and absorbing nutrients. Hence, if you have been eating less, start eating in the quantities and frequencies listed above in order to continue your healthy lifestyle.

Movement leads to strong immunity. Movement increases circulation, activating nutrient absorption and toxin release—the dual activities responsible for a good immune system. Do your stretches in the morning to rev up your circulation. Walk to earn your meals—10 minutes before breakfast, 10 minutes before lunch, 10 minutes before dinner and 15 minutes to half an hour after dinner. This way, even if you have a hectic schedule, without going to a gym or taking out time for a walk, you will be walking 45 minutes a day, which is wonderful for heart health and weight loss. The exercises written in the first three phases should not be let go just because you are now feeling cleansed.

Cheat once a week. When you have reached this far, it is important to reward yourself once a week as long as you don't overdo it. This gives you a feeling of being pampered and helps you stay guilt-free and disciplined for the rest of the week! Tips for eating out or ordering in are given in the next part.

Don't reuse oil. The once-a-week cheat meal can be anything you love—as long as it's not very large quantities and doesn't involve reheating oils. If you are frying something, discard leftover oil as reused oil increases your risk for cancer.

Walk for brain health. Walk while you talk on the phone! Walking increases immunity and makes your brain sharper. At work, this will help you finish tasks more efficiently.

Never forget your conscious breathing. Under all circumstances, being mindful about our breathing keeps inflammation levels from growing, the digestive system free from acid overload and helps maintain cortisol levels. Take out time every day to do your breathing exercises and if you cannot spare more time, do the one minute breathing exercise I have given in the next part at least four times a day. This will ensure that your shuddha foundation remains strong.

Chapter 5

Understanding Your Foods

We all know that we eat carbohydrates, proteins and fats. But what role do these play? And which are the good ones and which are the harmful ones? Let's break through the clutter and understand this so that every meal of yours is balanced with only healthy choices. Keep these points in mind when you are living the balanced life.

The first absolute truth for understanding your foods is: all calories aren't created equal.

1. The three major food groups are carbohydrates, proteins and fats.
2. Vegetables form a part of carbohydrates; however, due to their unrefined nature and higher number of nutrients, they are treated as a separate category.
3. Carbohydrates are also plant-based but are in a more processed form than vegetables. Carbohydrates give us energy, but in excess, they can give us diseases. Elimination of carbohydrates can cause chronic fatigue while excess of carbohydrates can invite type two diabetes, obesity, increased risk of inflammation, pessimism, mood disorders, depression and cancer.
4. Proteins give us strength and reduce fatigue. They also help build muscle; however, in excess, they can cause

kidney damage, brain fog and increase the acidic balance in the body.
5. Fats are important for the brain, digestion and joints. However, saturated fats will raise inflammation levels, can cause cholesterol and triglyceride deposits, fatty liver and invite heart disease.
6. In addition to this, water is the most important element that lubricates us, releases toxins, acts as a shock absorber, helps with circulation and absorption of nutrients, reduces fatigue, reduces blood pressure, prevents constipation and hydrates us. We are 70 per cent water; without water, we cannot survive.
7. Every nutrient you have heard of is present in carbohydrates, proteins, fats and water. Whether you hear about vitamins, minerals or micronutrients, all these are a part of carbohydrates, proteins and fats and it is water that enables their absorption in the human body. The most balanced way to eat your vitamins is to eat them through optimum-nutrition foods.

With the vast amount of choices available to us for food, what are the most optimum nutrition choices that will keep you balanced and healthy? Table number 2 will help you decide on better food choices once your detox is complete and help you live a life with a restored mind-body balance.

Table 2

State of Detox	Good Carbohydrates	Vegetables and Fruits	Fats	Proteins	Water and Beverages
If your gut is compromised	white rice, brown rice	all gourds, pumpkin, lettuce, potatoes, sweet potatoes, carrots, apple, pomegranate, musk melon, papaya	flaxseed oil, avocados, extra virgin olive oil	moong dal	one glass every 90 minutes of waking time, three green teas
When you have completed your shuddha programme	quinoa, oats, amaranth, white rice, brown rice, black rice, wild rice	all vegetables and low-sugar fruits, rotated as per availability and season	flaxseed oil, avocados, extra virgin olive oil, rice bran oil for cooking, nuts and seeds	moong dal, organic eggs, tofu, oily fish	one glass every 90 minutes of waking time, three green teas, fruit popsicles when thirsty, cucumber water
Once in 10 days	ragi, bajra, jowar, other millets	capsicum, bell peppers, eggplant	organic peanuts, cashew nuts	rajma, chana	fresh juices, lassi
Indulge in small quantities	dates, jaggery, organic honey	potatoes, beetroot, bananas, mangoes, chikus (sapodilla), watermelon, tomatoes, lime, lemon and sour items	butter, ghee	chicken, yoghurt, paneer, cheese, milk in tea or coffee	tea, coffee, coconut water, red wine, chaas

A note on the balance

My shuddha programme is a combination of clinical holistic nutrition which has been evidenced to heal chronic disease patients in combination with the principles of Ayurveda. With this powerful combination, staying cleansed is easier if you follow. However, some of the foods which are touted as healthy are going to upset the balance and you need to be mindful of consuming reduced quantities of these. I am putting down the explanation for these, so that you are aware of the right balance.

Lentils and pulses. All vegetarians look forward to lentils and pulses being their primary source of protein. However, in excess, lentils and pulses can get acidic. As per Ayurveda, the only lentil that does not cause mucus in the body is moong dal—the yellow one. Hence, consumption of this is the only thing permitted as part of lentil consumption during the detox programme. Reducing the amount of lentils and pulses once your balance is restored is a good way to keep your acid balance low. Especially pulses like Rajma and chana, which can cause bloating, acidity and reduce some of the effects of a cleansed digestive tract.

Sour items. Amlarasa (sour taste) is one of the main organoleptic entities in foods of the present day, which always tempts the consumer to indulge, every now and then. Balanced intake of amlarasa in a diet helps maintain functional health, but excessive intake produces signs and symptoms such as teeth hypersensitivity, stomatitis, halitosis, heartburn, urticaria, pimples, acne, joint inflammation and joint pain.

When our balance is restored, we can eat everything. However, as you refer to the table above, you will realize that there is a time and place to eat and drink. When 80 per cent of the time we live the detox life, we can indulge 20 per cent of the time. This makes the santosh (contentment) in our lives more balanced and we do not need to run to a harsh detox programme every few months. Any kind of overindulgence will cause imbalance. The primary focus of my shuddha programme is to help you stay balanced so that you can achieve a long and healthy life.

Chapter 6

Eating Shuddha Recipes

Many of us have forgotten the original taste of the food we eat because we douse them in so many masalas and overcook them. A large part of detoxification is eating clean foods and letting the natural flavours come out. In the recipes below, you will find that the natural flavours of the vegetables, herbs, seasoning and spices are light and melodious, and soon you will adapt to their delicious and mild flavours. As you shift from mindless eating to mindful eating, you will start noticing these flavours more strongly. When we are living mindlessly and not paying attention to the present, we need the crutch of lots of spices, sauces and overcooked food. But this is not required as we make our body shuddha and start living a healthier and cleaner life. Enjoy these recipes and watch yourself, step by step, become the best version of you.

Gut Cleansing Daily Gel Made with Aloe Vera and Water

Ingredients

2" x 2" leaf of aloe vera plant
1 glass room temperature drinking water

Method

Peel 2"x2" cut of aloe vera leaf, add half cup of water, blend in a mixer grinder, keep in the fridge. Take 1 tablespoon daily till it finishes. Make it fresh and you can store it for three to four days. You can increase quantities if your aloe vera plant does not make 1 tablespoon with a 2" x 2" cut of the leaf.

Take 1 tablespoon fresh aloe vera juice dissolved in it, along with 10 almonds (raw). Do not soak the almonds.

Coriander-Ginger Green Tea

Ingredients

Any good quality green tea leaves like Tulsi green tea or jasmine green tea
A bunch of well-washed coriander leaves, finely chopped
A sliver of sliced ginger, peeled, washed and crushed with juice
Organic honey

Method

Take the drinking water, put it in a pan on the gas and heat it. Switch off the flame just before it begins to boil. Do not boil the water. In a cup, add 1 teaspoon green tea leaves, finely chopped coriander leaves, crushed ginger with its juice and 1 tablespoon of organic honey. Add the hot water to the cup, cover the cup with a steel or glass lid—do not use plastic—and keep it covered for five minutes. Strain, stir and drink immediately.

Green Tea Masala for Evening Green Tea

Ingredients

1 teaspoon organic turmeric
10 cloves
10 cardamom pods
5 sticks of 2-inch-sized cinnamon
5 pieces aniseed
1 teaspoon freshly ground pepper
1 teaspoon fennel

Method

Put all the above ingredients together in a mixer and dry grind them to a powder and store. Take half a teaspoon of this powder and mix into the afternoon green tea daily. You can increase quantities in the above ratio to make a larger quantity of masala and store for longer in a glass jar. Do not use a plastic jar.

Poha

Ingredients

2 cups thick poha
1 tablespoon rice bran oil
1 teaspoon mustard seeds
1 teaspoon cumin seeds
Half teaspoon ground organic turmeric
8–10 curry leaves fresh or air dried
1 green chilly sliced lengthwise—optional
1 large onion diced finely
1 medium red or yellow potato peeled and diced small
Himalayan or sea salt to taste

Garnish

Half cup coriander finely chopped

Method

Rinse poha in a colander/seive under cold water, drain out all of the water and keep aside.

    Heat oil in a medium pan over high heat. Add the oil and mustard seeds. Allow the mustard seeds to pop. Once the mustard seeds start to pop, lower the heat to medium and add cumin seeds and cook until they start to sizzle, about 10 seconds. Next add curry leaves, green chillies, turmeric and mix well. Add onions, mix well and cook covered for two to three minutes on medium heat as they start to soften. Stir in potatoes, salt and cook covered until the potatoes are cooked through, about five minutes. Add poha and mix well and cook covered on low heat for five minutes or until poha is heated through. Garnish with coriander and enjoy hot.

Khichadi

Ingredients

Day 1: 5 florets of cauliflower, 10 pieces lauki/doodhi (bottle gourd), 4 leaves of any *one* of these as per availability: spinach/bathua/methi/sarson/colocasia/drumsticks/kulfa(purslane)/kalmi (water spinach)/haak (collard)/saunf patta/bok choy or any seasonal leaves that are available

Day 2: Half cup grated cabbage, half cup tori (ridge gourd), 4 leaves of any one of these as per availability: spinach/bathua/methi/sarson/colocasia/drumsticks/kulfa(purslane)/kalmi (water spinach)/haak (collard)/saunf patta/bok choy or any seasonal leaves that are available

Day 3: 1 carrot grated, 2 tindas peeled and grated, 4 leaves of any one of these as per availability: spinach/bathua/methi/sarson/colocasia/drumsticks/kulfa (purslane)/kalmi (water spinach)/haak (collard)/saunf patta/bok choy or any seasonal leaves that are available

Day 4: 1 tablespoon peas (fresh or frozen), 1 cup lauki, 4 leaves of any one of these as per availability: spinach/bathua/methi/sarson/Colocasia/drumsticks/kulfa (purslane)/kalmi (water spinach)/haak (collard)/saunf patta/bok choy or any seasonal leaves that are available

Day 5: 1 cup cut pumpkin (kaddu), 5 florets cauliflower or broccoli, 4 leaves of any one of these as per availability: spinach/bathua/methi/sarson/colocasia/drumsticks/kulfa (purslane)/kalmi (water spinach)/haak (collard)/saunf patta/bok choy or any seasonal leaves that are available

Day 6: 1 potato peeled and sliced in half, 10 leaves of any two of these as per availability: spinach/bathua/methi/sarson/colocasia/drumsticks/kulfa (purslane)/kalmi (water spinach)/haak (collard)/saunf patta/bok choy or any seasonal leaves that are available

Day 7: 1 carrot grated, 4 pieces parmal (pointed gourd) peeled and chopped, 4 leaves of any one of these as per availability: spinach/bathua/methi/sarson/colocasia/drumsticks/kulfa (purslane)/kalmi (water spinach)/haak (collard)/saunf patta/bok choy or any seasonal leaves that are available

For Tempering/Tadka

Day 1, 3, 6:

Half teaspoon turmeric
1 teaspoon cumin seeds
3 cloves
2 cardamom pods
Small stick of cinnamon
Half teaspoon ground pepper
1 chopped onion
1 tablespoon rice bran oil
3 cloves of garlic, 1 inch grated ginger
Water for cooking
Fresh coriander for garnishing
1 tablespoon extra virgin olive oil

Day 2, 4, 7:

Half teaspoon turmeric
1 teaspoon mustard seeds
10 curry leaves
3 cloves
2 cardamom
Small stick of cinnamon
Half teaspoon ground pepper
1 chopped onion
1 tablespoon rice bran oil
3 cloves of garlic
1 inch grated ginger
Water for cooking
Fresh coriander for garnishing
1 tablespoon extra virgin olive oil

Method

Wash 3 tablespoons of brown rice under running cold water till water runs clear. Soak them for 15–20 minutes. In this time, prepare everything else. Chop the veggies and keep them ready as per vegetable combinations and quantities listed in ingredients list.

In a pressure cooker, add 1 tablespoon rice bran oil, sauté the onions, add garlic, ginger, add 1 teaspoon cumin seeds or mustard seeds and curry leaves as per which day it is, other spices as per tadka ingredients listed. Stir-fry for one minute, add the vegetables, mix well and cook for two minutes. Now add rice. Make sure that you use the water you have soaked the rice in as that is rich in the water soluble vitamins and minerals. Add more water for loose consistency of khichdi. Mix and cook for two minutes. Add salt.

Cover the cooker with its lid, put the weight on. Cook on medium-high heat for two whistles, reduce the flame, cook on reduced flame for 20–25 minutes and turn off the gas. Allow the pressure cooker to cool down for 45 minutes and then open the lid. Mix all the ingredients together. If you feel that the water is less, add more water and give it another whistle. Khichdi is ready to serve. Serves up to two people. When you take 6–8 tablespoons in your bowl, add fresh chopped coriander and 1 tablespoon of extra virgin olive oil in that bowl. Do not heat the extra virgin olive oil or cook with it.

VEGETABLE SOUPS

Clear Vegetable Soup

Ingredients

2 cloves of garlic, finely chopped
Half teaspoon finely chopped ginger
1 onion, finely chopped
Half cup finely-chopped carrot, cabbage and french beans
1 teaspoon finely chopped fresh coriander
Salt, pepper, cinnamon to taste

Method

In a pan or pot, take 1 tablespoon of rice bran oil. Add garlic and ginger. Sauté until the raw aroma of both ginger and garlic goes away. Sauté for a few seconds, but do not brown them. Then add chopped onions; sauté until translucent. Add the cup of finely-chopped cabbage, carrots, french beans; sauté for one to two minutes on medium to low heat. Add water and allow it to simmer for seven to eight minutes by covering the pan. Season with one-fourth teaspoon ground black pepper or according to taste. Season with salt as needed. Sprinkle a pinch of cinnamon powder on the soup.

Carrot Soup

Ingredients

1 medium-sized carrot, peeled, washed, chopped
Half a medium-sized potato, peeled and chopped
2 tablespoons coriander leaves, washed well and chopped
2 cloves of garlic, finely chopped

Half a teaspoon finely chopped ginger
Half a teaspoon turmeric
A pinch of black pepper
Salt to taste
Half a medium-sized onion, finely chopped
1 tablespoon rice bran oil

Method

In a pressure cooker, add the carrot, potato and coriander leaves, add turmeric and 1 cup water. Close the lid, switch on the gas. Give it one whistle, reduce the flame, leave it on low flame for five minutes and switch off the gas. Do not touch for 30 minutes. During this time, you can make the tempering/tadka.

For tempering/tadka

In a pan, put rice bran oil, add onions and sauté till translucent. Add garlic and ginger and sauté for two more minutes.

After pressure cooker has cooled down, put everything in a mixer and make it into a pulp. Add water if consistency is too thick. Add this pulp to the tempering/tadka in the pan and simmer for two to three minutes. Add salt to taste. Soup is ready to serve!

Pumpkin/Bottle Gourd Soup

Ingredients

1 cup pumpkin or bottle gourd, peeled, washed, chopped into small pieces
1 medium-sized, finely-chopped onion
2 cloves of garlic, finely chopped
Half a teaspoon turmeric

A pinch of black pepper
Salt to taste
1 tablespoon rice bran oil

Method

In a pan, put rice bran oil, add onions and sauté till translucent. Add garlic and sauté for two more minutes. Add pumpkin/bottle gourd and stir-fry for five minutes and roast for another five minutes. Keep covering the pan in between for roasting. The water that drips from the lid of the pan should go inside the pan and should not be thrown away. Add a little bit of water during the roasting process if there is less water. Once pumpkin/bottle gourd looks like it is soft and roasted, switch off the gas and cover the pan. Allow it to cool. Once it has cooled, make it into a pulp/chutney in the mixer till it is blended completely smooth. Add one cup water and heat it. Roasted pumpkin soup is ready to eat!

Green Soup

Ingredients

1 stalk celery with leaves
4–5 leaves spinach or any other leaves available
1 bunch of freshly-washed coriander leaves
1 full chopped onion
1 green chilli
2 cloves of garlic
1 tablespoon rice bran oil
Salt and pepper to taste

Garnish

6 slivers of grated ginger

1 teaspoon mustard seeds
5 curry leaves
1 teaspoon rice bran oil

Method

In a pan, add 1 tablespoon rice bran oil. Add chopped onion, sauté till translucent, add garlic and green chilli. Sauté for five minutes. Add all the leaves and sauté for another five minutes. Switch off the flame and allow cooling by covering with lid. Once cooled, put it in a mixer and blend like chutney. Add one cup water, mix and heat. Add less water if you want thicker consistency. For garnishing, sauté one teaspoon mustard seeds, five curry leaves, grated ginger in one teaspoon rice bran oil and add over soup just before serving.

Garden Soup

Ingredients

1 carrot
Half cup cabbage
6–8 French beans
Half cup spinach
3 florets of cauliflower or 3 florets of broccoli

For Soup Base:

1 potato
Half an onion
Salt and pepper
4 cups water

For Tempering/Tadka:

Half inch piece ginger, grated

4 garlic cloves, grated
1 tablespoon rice bran oil

Garnish

1 tablespoon fresh coriander leaves

Method

Cook the soup base ingredients in the pressure cooker until well done. Then sauté the tempering ingredients in rice bran oil. Mix the soup base and tempering and press it through a sieve. Finely chop all the vegetables and cook in the soup base till tender. Add one cup water and simmer for five to seven minutes on low flame, cover the pan while doing so. Add salt and pepper and transfer to a cup/bowl, garnish with fresh coriander leaves. Serve hot.

Roasted Cauliflower Soup

Ingredients

5 medium-sized florets of cauliflower
One large onion, finely chopped
A bunch of fresh coriander leaves
1 tablespoon rice bran oil
Three cloves of garlic, minced
A pinch of cinnamon powder
Salt and pepper to taste

Method*

Chop the cauliflower into small pieces. In a ceramic pan, roast on low flame till evenly browned—it should be golden brown.

---

*You will need a high speed blender for this recipe.

Put aside to cool down. Put one tablespoon rice bran oil in a pan, add onions, sauté till translucent, then add minced garlic. Take a large bunch of coriander leaves and stir-fry for five minutes. Switch off the gas, allow cooling. Blend the roasted cauliflower with the rest of the ingredients until creamy smooth. Heat before serving. Add salt and pepper and season with a pinch of cinnamon powder before serving.

Important tip: This soup will come out tasty only if you roast the cauliflower well, therefore, ensure that you invest a lot of time and energy in roasting it on slow to medium flame, adjusting the flame as per the colour of the cauliflower.

Peas Soup

Ingredients

1 cup peas
2 mint sprigs
Half cup rice milk (recipe below)
1 medium, finely-chopped onion
4 cloves chopped garlic
Salt and pepper as required

Method

Boil the peas, cool and preserve the water. Sauté the garlic and onions in a pan until soft and brown. Add the peas and sauté for a few minutes and then cool. Blend the mixture and make a puree. Add 100 millilitres of rice milk and blend again. Heat the soup, garnish with mint sprigs, add salt and pepper and serve.

Moong Dal Soup/Broth

Ingredients

30 millilitres of varan (prepared as per recipe given in varan)
Half cup chopped French beans, cabbage and cauliflower/broccoli
Half cup drinking water

Method

In a pan, put the water, varan and vegetables together, bring to a boil and simmer for five to seven minutes till vegetables are semi soft. Do not overcook the vegetables. The mixture of varan and water will make the consistency of the soup medium to thin and the vegetables will add the crunchiness. You can add more varan or water as per the consistency you desire. Put in a bowl or a cup and enjoy. This is a wholesome moong dal and vegetable soup which will keep you satiated for long.

Rice Milk

Ingredients

Cooked brown rice—cooked in pressure cooker
Cheesecloth
Filtered Water

Method*

Rinse and cook brown rice in a pressure cooker so that all the water soluble nutrients are preserved. Use two tablespoons of cooked rice, three tablespoons water and add it to a high-

---

*You will need a high-speed blender for this recipe.

speed food processor/blender. Add half cup of water and blend again. Begin by blending for around 20 seconds, stop and check the consistency. Blend for longer if required. Ensure that there is enough water added for consistency after it is blended for it to become thin and creamy. Please remember: if you blended with a lot of water in the first instance, it will not be smooth. Hence, first you have to blend it to chutney/pulp consistency before you start adding small quantities of water to it. If you blend it for longer, till it's creamy, the rice grains disappear and it doesn't require filtering/sieving. Any sediment that is left in the milk isn't a good thing, so blend well. Two tablespoons of brown rice will give you 200 millilitres of brown rice milk.

Moong Dal Varan Recipe

Ingredients

100 grams yellow moong dal
An inch of ginger
2 cloves minced garlic
1 chopped onion
1 teaspoon organic turmeric powder
Sea or Himalayan salt to taste
Well-washed, chopped coriander leaves

For Tempering

1 tablespoon rice bran oil
1 heaped teaspoon of mustard seeds
10 curry leaves, well washed
Half a teaspoon cumin seeds
Pinch of organic asafoetida (hing)
1 tsp red chilli powder—optional

Method

Wash and soak moong dal in 3 cups of water for at least one hour. In a pressure cooker, add soaked dal along with water, ginger, chopped onion, turmeric powder and salt. Cover the pressure cooker with its lid. Cook the dal in the pressure cooker, cook for three to four whistles. Simmer on low heat and continue to cook for another 10 minutes. After 10 minutes, turn off the heat. Once the pressure cooker cools down, remove the lid and stir the dal. If the dal becomes blended and thick, add little water and stir it. The particles of the dal should not be visible and it should look like a blended smooth broth.

For tempering

Take a small pan, heat oil and add mustard seeds. Let the seeds crackle, then add cumin seeds, hing, curry leaves and red chilli powder. Switch off the flame to ensure that the spice mix doesn't get burned. Stir it and immediately pour the mixture in the dal. Stir and garnish with chopped coriander leaves. Serve hot with rice.

Boiled rice

Now you must be wondering why you need a boiled rice recipe. It's because this boiled rice is different from how you would normally make it, read below to understand.

Ingredients

1 cup kollam rice
2 cups water
1 teaspoon jasmine green tea leaves/jasmine flower and 2–3 leaves if you have the plant at home

1 clove of minced garlic
1 tablespoon extra virgin olive oil
Salt to taste

Method

Wash the rice well, put in a pressure cooker, add 2 cups of water, add jasmine green tea leaves, add minced garlic, give it one whistle, reduce the flame and let it cook for another five minutes. Switch off the flame and allow to cool for 30 minutes. Open the cooker, mix well, when you serve on your plate, add salt and 1 tablespoon extra virgin olive oil and mix well before you eat. This flavour will remind you of the ghee chawal flavour, except it does not have saturated fat and is extremely gut pacifying. This combination can also be used when you have severe acidity as it settles acidity and bloating. Serving size: 3 tablespoons for those above 75 kilos and 2 tablespoons for those below 70 kilos, to reduce acidity.

Nourishing Popsicles

Ingredients

1 fresh pomegranate, peeled and separated
1 tablespoon chia seeds
10 mint leaves
1 tablespoon ginger juice

Method

Crush fresh pomegranate and chia seeds, add mint leaves and make into a smoothie with less drinking water. After the smooth paste is made, dilute by adding more drinking water. Add 1 tablespoon ginger juice and mix well. Put the smoothie-drinking water mix into ice trays and freeze. These ice cubes should be put in 200 millilitres drinking water—they are nourishing and refreshing.

Tulsi Green Tea with Spices

It is best if you have a tulsi plant inside your house to make this tea. However, if you do not, you can purchase any organic brand of tulsi green tea.

Ingredients

6 leaves of tulsi
6 leaves of mint
10 leaves of coriander
1 tablespoon raw honey
Half a teaspoon organic turmeric
A pinch of black pepper
A pinch of clove powder

Method

Wash all the leaves well, crush them and put them in a ceramic cup, add black pepper, clove powder, organic honey and turmeric. Add hot—not boiling—water. Cover with a steel plate/glass cover for exactly five minutes. Open, stir well, strain and drink.

ROTIS

Methi Rotis

Ingredients

100 grams oats flour
2 tablespoons psyllium husk
1 medium-sized boiled potato

1 medium-sized onion, finely chopped
1 cup of well-washed and chopped methi leaves
A pinch of ajwain (caraway/carom seeds)
Green chillies (optional) and salt to taste
1 tablespoon extra virgin olive oil

Method

Knead oat flour with the boiled potato and psyllium husk; add ajwain, onions, methi leaves, green chillies and salt while kneading. The flour is soft and mouldable. Take some dry oat flour and use your hands, not the roller pin, to mould the roti. Make the roti seven to eight inches in diameter, not too thin, and shallow-roast on a granite or ceramic pan or iron tawa in less oil. Turn the side when golden brown. When the roti is cooked, put it on your plate, smear with extra virgin olive oil like you would smear ghee or butter. Enjoy!

Palak Rotis

Ingredients

100 grams quinoa flour
2 tablespoons white rice flour
2 tablespoons psyllium husk
1 medium-sized boiled potato
1 medium-sized onion, finely chopped
1 cup well-washed and chopped palak leaves
A pinch of ajwain (caraway/carom seeds)
Green chillies (optional) and salt to taste
1 tablespoon extra virgin olive oil

Method

Knead quinoa flour with the boiled potato and psyllium husk; add ajwain, onions, palak leaves, green chillies and salt while kneading. The flour is soft and mouldable. Take some dry rice flour and use your hands, not the roller pin, to mould the roti. Make the roti seven to eight inches in diameter, not too thin, and shallow-roast on a granite or ceramic pan or iron tawa in less oil. Turn the side when golden brown. When the roti is cooked, put it on your plate, smear with extra virgin olive oil like you would smear ghee or butter. Enjoy!

Brown Rice-Quinoa Rotis

Ingredients

1 tablespoon brown rice flour
1 tablespoon quinoa flour
1 tablespoon psyllium husk
Half an onion, chopped
A pinch of ajwain
Well-washed methi or coriander leaves
Salt and pepper to taste

Method

Make flour of brown rice and quinoa, store in glass jar. Take 1 tablespoon each and mix, per roti. Kneed and make flour. Add ajwain, salt, chopped onions, well-washed methi/coriander leaves and mix. Make into roti. The above quantity makes one roti, increase quantities in the same ratio to make more rotis.

Coriander Rotis

Ingredients

100 grams rice flour
2 tablespoons psyllium husk
1 medium-sized boiled potato
1 medium-sized onion, finely chopped
1 cup well-washed chopped coriander leaves
A pinch of ajwain (caraway/carom seeds)
Green chillis (optional) and salt to taste
1 tablespoon extra virgin olive oil

Method

Knead rice flour with the boiled potato and psyllium husk; add ajwain, onions, coriander leaves, green chillies and salt while kneading. The flour is soft and mouldable. Take some dry rice flour and use your hands, not the roller pin, to mould the roti. Make the roti seven to eight inches in diameter, not too thin, and shallow-roast on a granite or ceramic pan or iron tawa in less oil. Flip when golden brown. When the roti is cooked smear with extra virgin olive oil like you would smear ghee or butter. Enjoy!

CUT SALADS

Everybody knows cut salads and how to make them. So why am I giving you salad recipes? This is because these cut salads, which are going to start releasing your toxins, are different from the cut salads people have been having till now. Toxin build-up takes place when there is an absence of cut salads or raw items in our meal. These cut salad recipes are going to ensure that when combined with your meal, even later in your life, any daily toxins that get built up get released the very next day! Hence, addition of different kinds of cut salads are extremely important.

Cut Salad—Kuchumber

Traditionally common in North India, especially Punjab, this variation has been tweaked to release your toxins and make your digestive system shuddha!

Ingredients

Half a cucumber, finely chopped
Half an onion, finely chopped
A bunch of coriander leaves, well washed and finely chopped
5 mint leaves, well washed and chopped
Salt and pepper to taste
1 green chilli thinly sliced—optional
1 tablespoon extra virgin olive oil

Method

Mix all the ingredients together, toss them well and refrigerate for 45 minutes before eating. Perfect for the summer, it also reduces virus activities in the body. Serves one.

Cut Salad Patta

Ingredients

A bunch of coriander leaves, well washed and finely chopped
10 mint leaves, well washed and chopped
Well-washed 5 to 10 leaves (depending upon size, for smaller leaves take 10, for larger leaves take 5) of any available salad leaves or leafy vegetables—choose from spinach, bathua, lettuce, salaad patta, curry leaves

1 clove minced garlic
Salt and pepper to taste
1 green chilli thinly sliced—optional
1 tablespoon extra virgin olive oil

Method

Mix all ingredients together, toss them well, refrigerate for 45 minutes before eating. Perfect for the summer, it reduces virus and bacterial activities in the body and gut, infuses the digestive system with good bacteria. Serves one.

Delicious tip: You can also make this into a chutney by adding a little bit of drinking water and wet grinding it. Add this as chutney for better flavour to your food!

Cut Salad—Bhaji

This salad is made by very lightly stir-frying vegetables for just a couple of minutes to maintain their crunchiness. It is important that we eat our vegetables semi-raw to preserve their nutrients.

Ingredients

Half a cup of cabbage, shredded
Half a carrot, shredded
Half an onion, sliced
3 medium-sized cloves of garlic, peeled
10 curry leaves
1 teaspoon mustard seeds
Salt and pepper to taste
1 green chilli thinly sliced—optional
1 tablespoon rice bran oil
1 tablespoon extra virgin olive oil

Method

In a pan, heat one tablespoon rice bran oil and crackle mustard seeds and curry leaves. Add garlic, stir-fry on high flame for one minute till garlic turns golden brown, add onions, stir-fry for one to two minutes till they sweat out the water, add carrots and cabbage and stir-fry for five minutes. Add salt and pepper, one green chilli, switch off the gas and cover with a lid. Allow it to cook in its own steam for 30 minutes. This process is extremely important—after switching off the gas, it is critical that the pan is covered completely and there is condensation that takes place for 30 minutes. Open the lid, let the water in condensation mix with the preparation, then transfer to a bowl, cover and refrigerate for 30 minutes before eating.

Brown Rice Sauté

Ingredients

Half cup chopped beans
Half cup broccoli/cauliflower
Half cup grated carrot
Half cup shredded cabbage
Rock/sea salt as per taste
A pinch of thyme, rosemary and oregano. If these are not available, then add coriander leaves or parsley
Half teaspoon crushed garlic
1 medium-sized, chopped onion
A pinch of turmeric powder
A pinch of black pepper
5 almonds
5 tablespoon boiled brown rice
1 teaspoon rice bran oil
3–4 tablespoon extra virgin olive oil

Method

Steam the veggies in a steamer or pressure cooker for 10 minutes. In a ceramic or steel pan, add oil and sauté crushed garlic, chopped onions, steamed veggies, turmeric, black pepper, salt and herbs. Once done, switch off the flame and mix 5 tablespoon of boiled brown rice.

When on the plate, sprinkle sliced almonds and pour 3–4 tablespoon of extra virgin oil on top of it.

Note: Do not cook/roast/heat the almonds as they lose their good fat content.

Vegetable Pulao in a Pressure Cooker

Wash the 3 tablespoons of brown rice or quinoa under running cold water till water runs clear. Take that in a large bowl and add enough water. Soak for 15–20 minutes. In this time, prepare everything else as below.

Preparatory Steps

Chop the veggies and keep them ready in the following quantities:
1 cup cauliflower or broccoli (vary taste by alternating these)
Half cup cabbage
1 carrot
1 tablespoon peas (fresh or frozen)
1 cup doodhi/torai (bottle/ridge gourd) (vary taste by alternating these)
1 potato peeled and sliced in half

After soaking brown rice for 15 minuntes, discard the water and keep it aside.

Method

In a pressure cooker, add 1 tablespoon rice bran oil, add and sauté the onions, add 4 cloves of garlic, 1 teaspoon cumin seeds, 1 teaspoon methi seeds, 1 teaspoon kasoori methi, half teaspoon turmeric, a pinch of black pepper, a couple of cloves, 1 bay leaf and 2 cardamom pods. After they have tempered for a couple of minutes, add the vegetables, mix well and cook for two minutes. Mix again. Now add the drained rice. Mix and cook for two minutes. Add two cups of water and salt.

Cover the cooker with lid, put the weight on. Cook on medium-high heat for two whistles, reduce the flame, cook on reduced flame for 10 minutes and turn off the stove. Allow the pressure cooker to cool down for 45 minutes and then open the lid. Fluff up the rice and add whole spices using a fork.

Veg pulao is ready to serve. Serves one to two people.

Coriander Curry

Ingredients

A large bunch of coriander, freshly washed and chopped
3 onions, peeled
5 garlic cloves, peeled
2 centimetres sliced ginger, well chopped
10 curry leaves
1 teaspoon cumin seeds
2 green chillies, slit lengthwise
Half teaspoon organic turmeric powder
1 tablespoon rice bran oil
Salt and pepper to taste

Method

Chop the onions, ginger and garlic and put in a ceramic pan, add a tablespoon of oil and stir-fry all three together till golden brown, add coriander leaves. Stir fry for five minutes, switch off gas. Cool the mixture down. Make into a paste by adding water in a mixer-grinder. Put aside. In a small pan, add one tablespoon rice bran oil, add curry leaves and cumin seeds and add green chillies and turmeric. Stir-fry for five minutes. Add salt and pepper, mix with the paste. Put this paste in the pressure cooker and dilute with water to make it into a base for vegetable curry, with vegetables of your choice or combined with pulao.

Curry Vegetable

In phase two, it is important that you have one curry vegetable and one dry vegetable. Increasing quantities of vegetables is not as difficult as it seems! With the presence of a curry vegetable, we do not miss out on other heavy curries which can cause toxins like high triglycerides and put pressure on the liver. A thin curry with partially cooked vegetables is ideal to protect the nutrients and make the vegetables do the releasing of toxins!

Ingredients

1 medium-sized onion, chopped finely
3 cloves of garlic, minced into paste
1 teaspoon ginger paste
1 teaspoon cumin seeds
Half teaspoon turmeric
A pinch of black pepper
1 tablespoon rice bran oil

Method

Heat the iron or ceramic pan, add rice bran oil, add onions and stir-fry for a minute till they sweat it out. Add ginger and garlic paste and sauté till they are golden brown. Add cumin seeds and roast for another five minutes. Add turmeric and black pepper. Keep adding small quantities of water as the paste becomes brown or starts sticking to the pan to make it into a thick paste. Once it is roasted brown, switch off the gas and allow the mixture to cool. Then, in a blender, blend it completely and add water as per consistency of curry required in the vegetable.

Put this entire mixture in a pressure cooker, add three vegetables as per availability and choice. You can choose from the following list:

- Cabbage
- Cauliflower
- Carrots
- French beans
- Bottle gourd
- Ridge gourd
- Tinda or Indian squash
- Kaddu or pumpkin
- Shakarkandi or sweet potato

Spinach leaves—don't add these leaves in a pressure cooker as they cook very fast. When you are making the curry, you can add the spinach to the last part of the roasting and then blend it in a mixer. This makes a nice broth and you can put seasoning or tadka over it with 1 teaspoon of rice bran oil, 4–5 curry leaves and a teaspoon of mustard seeds.

Except for spinach, you can add any three vegetables from the above list and rotate different vegetables every day. This way you will get your nutrients. Cook till one whistle goes off and then switch off the flame. Allow the pressure cooker to cool down for 30 minutes before you open. This is important to preserve the water soluble vitamins.

Roasted Makhanas

Makhanas are rich in good fat; they are a light and delicious Indian snack. This preparation can be stored in a glass jar and had as and when you want to.

Ingredients

250 grams makhanas
1 tablespoon mustard seeds
15 curry leaves
Half a teaspoon organic turmeric
A pinch of black pepper
Salt to taste
1 tablespoon rice bran oil

Method

Take a deep iron or ceramic kadhai and heat it. Add one tablespoon rice bran oil, add mustard seeds and curry leaves and crackle them. Add turmeric, black pepper and stir. Add makhanas and roast on a slow flame till golden brown. Switch off the gas and keep roasting since the pan must still be hot—for another five minutes. Allow it to cool. After it has cooled down, add salt. Add salt only at the end as it can make the makhanas soggy if added earlier.

Murmura Bhel

Ingredients

250 grams murmura or puffed rice
1 tablespoon mustard seeds
15 curry leaves
50 grams roasted organic peanuts
6 small cloves of garlic
Half a teaspoon organic turmeric
A pinch of black pepper
Salt to taste
1 tablespoon rice bran oil

Method

Take a deep iron or ceramic kadhai and heat it. Add one tablespoon rice bran oil, add mustard seeds and curry leaves and crackle them. Add garlic and cook till golden brown. Add turmeric and black pepper and stir. Add murmura and roast on a high flame for just five minutes. Switch off the gas and keep roasting till the pan is hot—for another five minutes. Allow it to cool. Add roasted peanuts. After it has cooled down, add salt. Add the salt only at the end as it can make the murmure soggy if added earlier.

Note: It is important to roast the peanuts separately and add later. Otherwise the peanuts can be under or overcooked and interfere with the flavours of garlic, curry leaves and mustard seeds.

Roasted Chivda

Ingredients

250 grams thin poha
1 tablespoon mustard seeds
15 curry leaves
50 grams roasted organic peanuts
6 small cloves of garlic
Half a teaspoon organic turmeric
A pinch of black pepper
Salt to taste
1 tablespoon rice bran oil

Method

Take a deep iron or ceramic kadhai and heat it. Add one tablespoon of rice bran oil, add mustard seeds and curry leaves and let them crackle in the oil. Add garlic and cook till golden brown. Add turmeric and black pepper and stir. Add poha and roast on a high flame for just five minutes. Switch off the gas and keep roasting till the pan is hot—for another five minutes. Allow to cool. Add roasted peanuts. After it has cooled down, add salt. Add salt only at the end as it can make the poha soggy if added earlier. Once it has cooled down, your crisp and crunchy snack is ready! Store in glass jar.

Note: It is important to roast the peanuts separately and add later. Otherwise the peanuts can be under or overcooked and interfere with the flavours of garlic, curry leaves and mustard seeds.

Oat Milk

Ingredients

3 tablespoons rolled oats
200 millilitres of filtered drinking water

Method

Add the oats, water and any additional sweeteners to a high powered blender. Then blend for 20–30 seconds (make sure not to over blend).

Strain the mixture. Pour it through a nut milk bag or a thin cheesecloth over a large mixing bowl or pitcher. You'll want to double strain the mixture to make sure all the sediment is removed.

Store the oat milk. Transfer the oat milk to a sealed glass container and store it in the fridge. You can make a larger quantity, to last you the entire week.

Almond Milk Thandai

Ingredients

200 millilitres of almond milk
1 tablespoon khus
1 tablespoon pomegranate
1 tablespoon chia seeds
2 green cardamom pods, crushed
1 date, deseeded

Method

Blend 30 millilitres of almond milk with one tablespoon each of khus, pomegranate, chia seeds and two cardamom pods in a mixer. It will form a thick coarse paste. Then add the remaining almond milk and blend again for two minutes. Refrigerate it and make it cold. Thandai is ready!

Moong Dal Omelette

Ingredients

Half an onion, chopped
One-fourth capsicum, chopped
Half a ripe tomato, chopped
2 button mushrooms, finely chopped
Fresh coriander leaves, well washed and chopped finely
2 large garlic cloves (minced)
Salt and black pepper
1 green chilli, finely chopped—optional
1 tablespoon rice flour (grind at home)
2 tablespoons moong dal flour (grind at home)
1 tablespoon rice bran oil

Method

Mix the rice flour and moong dal flour in 25 millilitres of water, so that it becomes a thin but smooth paste. Keep aside and allow to ferment for 30 minutes. Check after 30 minutes; if it is too thick, add more water for it to have batter consistency. In a granite saucepan, add one tablespoon of rice bran oil. Put all the vegetables, green chilli and seasoning such as garlic, coriander, salt and pepper and stir-fry for two to three minutes. Reduce the flame and add the flour mix into the veggies and let it spread. The thinner it is, the more evenly you can spread it. When it is brown, flip the side. Make it crispy and golden brown. Serve with tomato chutney.

Tomato Chutney

This traditional salsa is lacto-fermented, so it stays good for a very long time and has a great fuzzy and pungent taste.

Ingredients

4 fresh tomatoes, chopped
1 onion, finely chopped
3 dried chillies, whole
4 garlic cloves, minced
A pinch of sea salt
50 grams organic peanuts
Half teaspoon turmeric
A pinch of black pepper
1 teaspoon mustard seeds
15 curry leaves
Salt to taste
1.5 tablespoons rice bran oil

Method

Heat 1 tablespoon rice bran oil in an iron or ceramic pan, add chopped onions, sauté for two minutes till they sweat. Add minced garlic and dried chillies, sauté for another two minutes. Add chopped, fresh tomatoes and sauté for two minutes. Reduce the flame and keep punching the tomatoes to make them pulpy. Add turmeric and black pepper. You may need to sprinkle some water in order to cook the tomatoes partially. After five minutes of doing this, switch off the flame and keep aside. Take 50 grams of organic peanuts, roast them and keep aside. Then in a blender, add organic peanuts and tomato pulp and wet grind till absolutely smooth. You may need to add water for the consistency you require. Taste and add salt. Now is the time for tadka! In an iron pan, add half tablespoon of rice bran oil, mustard seeds and curry leaves and let them crackle. Add this tadka to the tomato chutney before serving!

Quinoa Upma

Ingredients

50 grams raw white quinoa
1 onion, finely chopped
1–2 dried chillies, whole—optional
4 garlic cloves, chopped
A pinch of sea salt
12–15 organic roasted peanuts
Half teaspoon turmeric
A pinch of black pepper
1 teaspoon mustard seeds
15 curry leaves
1 tablespoon rice bran oil

Method

Take 50 grams of raw quinoa and 250 millilitres of water, put it in a pressure cooker and after one whistle, reduce the flame and cook for 20 minutes. Allow the pressure cooker to cool. In the meantime, roast peanuts and keep aside. Then take an iron or ceramic pan, add 1 tablespoon rice bran oil, add onion, sauté till they sweat for two minutes, add mustard seeds, curry leaves and sauté till they crackle, then add garlic, chillies, turmeric, black pepper and salt. Sauté for two minutes and then reduce the flame. Open the pressure cooker, take the boiled quinoa and add to this tadka. In case you need to evaporate some of the water in the quinoa, you can cook for five to seven minutes. Quinoa upma is high in fibre and protein and will keep you nourished and content as a wonderful breakfast or snack item!

Oats Upma

Ingredients

50 grams oat flour—dry grind at home
1 onion, finely chopped
Half a potato, cut into small cubes
1–2 dried chillies, whole—optional
4 garlic cloves, chopped
A pinch of sea salt
12–15 organic roasted peanuts
1 tablespoon channa dal
Half teaspoon turmeric
A pinch of black pepper
1 teaspoon mustard seeds
15 curry leaves
1.5 tablespoons rice bran oil

Method

Take 50 grams of oat flour in a bowl; add water to make the consistency smooth and without lumps. Keep aside. In the meantime, roast peanuts and keep aside. Then take an iron or ceramic pan, add one tablespoon of rice bran oil. Add onions, sauté till they sweat, for two minutes, then add chana dal and roast for five minutes. Add potatoes, garlic, chillies, turmeric, black pepper and salt. Sauté for two to three minutes. Reduce the flame. Slowly add the oat flour so that it can blend into the tadka. Add water for a loose consistency and simmer for seven to 10 minutes on low flame while keeping it covered. Check if potatoes are cooked, switch off the flame. Make sure that the oats upma is not thick and has a slightly loose consistency as this is enjoyed better. Now is the time for tadka! In an iron pan, add half a tablespoon of rice bran oil, add mustard seeds and curry leaves and let them crackle. Throw this tadka on the oats upma before serving! Oats upma is high in fibre and protein and will keep you nourished and content as a wonderful breakfast or snack item!

Oats Porridge

Ingredients

50 grams oats flour—dry grind at home
200 millilitres almond milk
2 dates, deseeded
Water for consistency

Method

Take 50 grams of oat flour in a bowl; add water to make consistency smooth and without lumps. Keep aside. Take a steel or ceramic pan and put the almond milk to boil. When it starts to boil, reduce the flame and slowly start adding the dissolved oat flour in the almond milk. If it gets too thick, add water. Ensure that no lumps are formed. Simmer on a low flame for seven to 10 minutes. Add one or two dates as per the sweetness requirement and let the dates melt and blend into the oats porridge. Keep adding water to reach the consistency you need. Serve hot. This porridge is high in protein and fibre and is an instant energy lifter!

Tofu Bhurji

Ingredients

200 grams fresh soya paneer
One medium-sized onion, finely chopped
A bunch of well-washed coriander leaves, finely chopped
2 green chillies, finely chopped—optional
1 teaspoon cumin seeds
Half a teaspoon turmeric
A pinch of black pepper
Sea salt to taste
1 tablespoon rice bran oil

Method

Take the soya paneer and crumble it with your hands. Keep aside and cover. In a ceramic or iron pan, add the rice bran oil, onions and cumin seeds and sauté for two minutes. Add green chillies, chopped coriander, turmeric, black pepper and salt and sauté for one minute, add the crumbled soya paneer and stir for two to three minutes till everything is mixed together and the soya paneer gets the golden glow of the turmeric. Bhurji is ready!

The following recipes are additional to what you have been prescribed from phase one to phase three. These recipes can be utilized to give you variety and flavour starting phase four so that your detoxification remains intact while you leave your new normal.

Protein-Rich Vegetable Rice

Ingredients

Half a cup brown rice
Half a cup white rice
1 big onion, thinly sliced
3 cups mixed vegetables (beans, cauliflower, cabbage, carrot—cut in cubes)
Three-fourth cup almond milk
8 mint leaves
1 tablespoon coriander leaves
Half teaspoon turmeric powder
5 pepper corns

For Grinding

1 tablespoon fennel seeds
4 cloves garlic
1 green chilli
1 teaspoon mace
2 tablespoon water

For Tempering

1 tablespoon rice bran oil
1 piece cinnamon
4 cloves
2 cardamom pods
4 bay leaves

Method

Heat one tablespoon of oil in a pressure cooker. Add all the ingredients under tempering. Add the chopped onion and sauté it till the raw smell goes away. Add the ground mixture; let it cook until the raw smell goes away. Add all the vegetables, turmeric, peppercorns, mint and coriander leaves. Mix well for one minute, add rice, three-fourth cup of almond milk and three-fourth cup of water. Add salt.

Cook in the pressure cooker for 20 minutes on low flame. Switch off the flame and keep to cool for 30 minutes. Open and enjoy! This is a wonderful, filling lunch for vegetarians who cannot add eggs or fish to their meal plan. The almond milk provides richness and proteins.

Rice-Stuffed Cabbage Rolls

Ingredients

3 or 4 leaves of cabbage
2 cups cooked brown and white rice mixed
Half cup finely chopped onions
1 cup broccoli
1 cup finally chopped carrots
1 cup finally chopped French beans
1 pinch of black pepper
One-fourth teaspoon jeera
1 clove minced garlic
One-fourth teaspoon organic turmeric powder
Salt to taste

Method

Cook brown and white rice in an equal proportion. Sauté the onion, garlic, broccoli, carrots and French beans in very little rice bran oil. Add salt, turmeric and black pepper to it. For the tadka, take a small amount of rice bran oil, add the jeera and switch off the flame once the jeera starts crackling. Add this tadka to the boiled brown and white rice mixture. Keep it aside. Sauté the vegetables with one teaspoon rice bran oil. Keep aside. Blanch the cabbage by putting it in hot boiling water for just one minute and then immerse it in cold water to maintain the colour of the leaves. Spread the cabbage leaves, trim the thick vein from the bottom of each cabbage leaf making a V-shaped cut. Spread a layer of rice over it.

Add the sautéed vegetables over it, keeping in mind the rice to vegetables proportion of 1:1. Pull the cut edges of the leaf together to overlap, fold over the filling, fold in the sides and roll up.

Protein tip: In case you need to up your protein intake, instead of the brown and white rice combination, you can add crumbled tofu or tofu bhurji and roll up the cabbage leaves!

Non-Lentil Muthiya

Ingredients

100 grams rice or quinoa flour
1 teaspoon ginger-garlic homemade paste
1 teaspoon green chilli homemade paste
Half a gourd, grated
A pinch of whole spices as per taste
1 teaspoon mustard seeds
1 teaspoon sesame seeds

Method

Grate the bottle gourd (lauki/doodhi). Mix the rice flour (or quinoa flour if you're diabetic), with fresh homemade green chilli paste, ginger-garlic paste and add salt to taste. Mix the grated gourd and the flour mix, and use water to make long rolls. It will be semi-solid. Place them on the plate and steam it for 20–30 minutes. Once it is cooked, take it off. Allow it to cool, cut into pieces and then sauté it in oil, sesame seeds and whole spices of your choice.

Gingered Nuts (Sweet and Salty)

Ingredients

3 cups mixed nuts, unsalted
2 tablespoons sesame seeds
6 tablespoons organic jaggery, powdered
3 teaspoons ginger juice
One-fourth teaspoon red chilli powder
One-fourth teaspoon ground black pepper
1 teaspoon black salt
4 tablespoons water

Method

Preheat the oven. While it heats, make a jaggery syrup by mixing jaggery and water and bringing it to a boil, stirring occasionally, until the jaggery dissolves. Combine nuts, red chilli powder, black pepper, black salt and sesame seeds and keep aside. Pour jaggery syrup over nut mixture and toss well. Line a baking tray with butter paper and arrange nuts in a single layer on it. Bake until golden at 150°C for 15–20 minutes, stirring occasionally. Cool and break into bite-size pieces.

Note: Since the smoke point of nut oil is 200°C, keeping it lower than that still preserves the good fat in them.

Egg Salad with Tulsi Leaves

Ingredients

2 organic eggs, hard boiled and quartered
1 carrot, chopped
1 fennel head, chopped
1 garlic clove, grated
2 tablespoons extra virgin olive oil
A handful of tulsi leaves
Pepper, freshly ground
Salt to taste

Method

Wash tulsi leaves well, crush them with a silwatta (mortar and pestle). Add the extra virgin olive oil, garlic, salt and pepper. This becomes a thick dressing. Take the eggs, slice each egg into four pieces, drizzle the dressing on top and toss. Serve cold. The uncooked tulsi leaves will increase immunity and release toxins and the organic eggs will provide energy and heal thyroid problems.

Saag Paneer

Ingredients

2 tablespoons rice bran oil
1 teaspoon organic turmeric
1 teaspoon organic chilli powder—optional
450 grams tofu, cut into 3-centimetre cubes
500 grams spinach
1 large onion, finely chopped
3 garlic cloves

1 thumb-sized piece of ginger
1 green chilli, roughly chopped (include seeds for extra spice)—optional
1 teaspoon home-made garam masala
Half lemon, juiced, to serve

Method

Place spinach in a metal sieve (colander), wash well by pouring boiling water over it, drain and cool, then put in a tea towel and squeeze out most of the water. Chop roughly.

Stir-fry the onion with the garlic, ginger and green chilli. Cook the tofu in a large frying pan over high heat for around five minutes (it has to be high heat so that the tofu can be quickly cooked without crumbling, as it is softer than paneer), toss the pan so they become golden all over. Remove and set aside on a plate, leaving the spices behind in the pan. Add the onion mix to the pan, add a pinch of salt and turn the heat down. Fry until caramel coloured, for around 10 minutes, add a splash of water if it looks a little dry. Add the garam masala and stir-fry for two minutes. Add the spinach and cook for further two to three minutes, adding 100 millilitres of water to release all the flavour from the bottom of the pan. Add the tofu and cook for two to three minutes. This recipe preserves some of the antioxidants of spinach much more as you are not first completely boiling it and then simmering it. Overcooking and overheating of the spinach kills the iron content in it. Replacing paneer with tofu reduces the number of calories that you consume and it is very high in antioxidants.

Rice Noodles

This is a wonderful treat to give yourself without derailing your shuddha life. It is also wonderful to make it for the entire family as kids enjoy it too!

Ingredients

Rice noodles (look for those without any additives or preservatives in your supermarket, they are easily available)
1 red/yellow peppers or capsicum as per availability, finely sliced
1 onion, finely sliced
6–7 garlic cloves, peeled and ground coarsely
1 carrot, shredded
One-fourth medium-sized cabbage, thinly sliced
Sesame oil (the Chinese one, not the Indian til ka tel)
Black pepper
Chilli flakes—optional
Salt to taste

Method

Take 2.5 litres of water and bring it to a boil, add the rice noodles, stir for five minutes and switch off the gas. Rice noodles take very little time to cook so make sure that you are monitoring it even for these five to seven minutes. Take a metal sieve, put it on top of a pan near the sink, and drain out the water from the rice noodles. Wash the rice noodles with cold running tap water, put aside and cover.

In a ceramic pan, put some sesame oil, add the chopped capsicum or red and yellow peppers, onions and garlic. Stir-fry for five minutes, add the shredded cabbage and carrots, stir-fry for another five minutes, add salt to taste, switch off the gas and cover tightly. Leave the vegetables in the covered pan with the gas off for 10 minutes. This helps absorption of water-soluble vitamins better. After 10 minutes, switch on the gas again, open the lid, add the black pepper and chilli flakes and stir in the rice noodles. Mix them well while they are still on the gas. Mix with two wooden ladles with both hands so that the rice noodles are handled delicately and do not break too much. Switch off the gas. Your vegetable rice noodles is ready to serve. The sesame oil would have added a nutty, Chinese flavour to the entire dish and the vegetables are crunchy and full of antioxidants.

Gluten-Free Pizza

Ingredients

Pizza base (recipes below)
Tomato paste (recipe below)
Almond cheese (recipe available in later in this section)
Extra virgin olive oil
Chopped vegetables of choice

Method

Make the pizza base as per the recipe below. Spread the tomato sauce over the pizza crust, brush the crust with a bit of olive oil here if you'd like a darker crust. Add vegetables like finely-chopped mushrooms and broccoli and almond cheese and bake it for about 20 minutes at 200°C in the oven.

Remove from the oven and allow the pizza to cool slightly before serving. Serve hot and enjoy!

Popular Topping Combinations

Broccoli florets, black olives, roasted garlic, sun-dried tomatoes, fresh tomatoes, fresh basil leaves, chopped bell peppers, chopped onions, fresh herbs and marinated artichoke hearts. Or you can add your own!

Pizza Base

Ingredients

2 large potatoes
One-third cup warm water
1 tablespoon honey
7–8 grams (a heaped teaspoon) package dry yeast
1 cup white rice flour
Half a cup tapioca starch
Salt
1 large egg white
1 tablespoon extra virgin olive oil

Method

Boil the potatoes in a pressure cooker. After the cooker has cooled down, open it. Once the potatoes are cool enough to handle, remove the skin and mash them. Set aside. Stir the warm water, honey and yeast in a measuring cup or small bowl. Let it sit for three to five minutes until a small layer of foam develops at the top. If this doesn't happen, discard and try again with new yeast. Add the potatoes, rice flour, tapioca starch and three-fourth teaspoon of salt in a bowl. Mix/knead by hand or in a food processor on medium speed until the mixture is combined and forms a fine, crumbly meal. Continuing to mix on medium, add the egg white and olive oil; slowly drizzle in the yeast mixture and mix until the dough comes together. Cover the bowl tightly with a wrap and set in a warm place until the dough increases by half. This should take about one and a half hours.

Cauliflower Pizza Base

Ingredients

2 cups cauliflower, riced/grated
1 teaspoon dried oregano
1 teaspoon dried parsley
1 garlic clove, minced
1 egg, beaten
Half a cup grated vegan cheese
2 tablespoons olive oil
Sea salt
Freshly ground black pepper

Method

Preheat oven to 200°C. Fill a saucepan with about an inch of water, and bring it to a light boil over medium-high heat. Add the grated cauliflower and let it cook for four to five minutes. Drain the water from the saucepan, and use a dish towel or cheesecloth to drain the cauliflower completely, squeezing it tightly. Remove as much water as possible. Once the cauliflower has cooled down, mix in a bowl with the dried oregano, dried parsley, garlic, beaten egg, olive oil and season to taste. Place the dough on a pizza tray lined with parchment paper, and shape it into a round shape. Bake in the oven for 15–20 minutes.

Tomato Sauce

Ingredients

2.5 kilograms tomatoes
1 teaspoon fine sea salt
Half to 1 cup extra virgin olive oil

Half teaspoon pepper
1 teaspoon oregano
A pinch of crushed red pepper

Method

Chop the tomatoes into four parts, and put them in a pot over the gas. Add half a cup of water. Bring the tomatoes to a boil over high heat. Cook by stirring just until the tomatoes soften, for about two minutes. This brief cooking helps break the tomatoes down a bit and make them easier to run through a sieve. Switch off the gas. Add about half a cup of the olive oil and one teaspoon of fine sea salt to the tomatoes and wet grind into a paste. In a medium saucepan, combine the garlic, salt and tomato paste along with the sauce and sugar, pepper, oregano, olive oil and crushed red pepper. Blend well and bring to a simmer. Reduce the heat to low and continue cooking, stirring frequently, for about three to four minutes. Let the sauce cool down.

Almond Cheese (Vegan)

Ingredients

1 cup whole raw unsalted almonds (skin removed; see notes about blanching and/or soaking almonds below)
3 tablespoons lemon juice
3 tablespoons extra virgin olive oil
A pinch each of oregano and black pepper
2 garlic cloves, crushed
Three-fourth teaspoon salt
Half a cup water
Dried herbs like oregano, thyme, rosemary

Method

Boil some water, switch off the gas, soak the almonds in the boiling hot water for 20 minutes. Drain and rinse the almonds, then either rub them with a towel or just use your fingers to peel and pop the skin off. Soak the blanched almonds in cold water for 24 hours. Cover and refrigerate for 24 hours. Drain and rinse the almonds well. Put the almonds in a mixer grinder or a high-powered blender with the lemon juice, olive oil, salt and water. Blend until smooth.

Use a double-layered cheesecloth or a fine handkerchief to drain the mixture. Scrape the mixture into the cloth. Add the dried herbs, pepper, salt and crushed garlic and mix it well. Gather the cloth tightly around the almond mixture and make a bundle by using a rubber band or string to tie the top. Give the bundle a few gentle squeezes to remove the liquid.

Leave the bundle in a metal sieve with the water draining in another container below it and put in the refrigerator overnight over a bowl or rimmed plate to catch any liquid that might drain. Refrigerate for 12 hours. This helps firm the texture of the cheese. Discard any liquid that drains out. Carefully peel the cloth off the almond cheese. The cheese will have a consistency similar to cake dough. If you like it fresh, you can eat it in this form as soft cheese, or gently shape it into a square container and bake it at 150°C for 30–40 minutes. After baking, the top will be dry and slightly firm. The inside will still be creamy. The flavours of salt, garlic, herbs and black pepper will make this cheese even tastier.

Note: Even though I don't recommend soaking and removing the skin of almonds, having vegan cheese is a far healthier option, so we can take this liberty. Removing the skin before making almond cheese gives the cheese a smoother texture and lighter colour that makes it look like dairy cheese. You can make the cheese with the skin on if you prefer that.

PART THREE

Emotional Detox

Without purity, no intellectual progress is possible.

Chapter 1

Toxins and Stress

Hello, you beautiful person! The shuddha programme has helped you inculcate mindfulness in your food and eating habits. If you have reached this far, your understanding of what you need to eat in order to release your toxins has become sound. However, did you know that you are only 50 per cent of the way there? Most of us accumulate toxins in our body because of our level of stress. Stress is everywhere—so how do you protect yourself from it? We cannot make stress disappear. But we can regulate our response to stress.

We learnt how to release daily food toxins by following the right habits and combinations. This helps us regulate our bowel movements, stay calm and have higher energy and glowing skin. This calmness we experienced was just the trailer. A major part of leading a shuddha life means more positive moods. Positive moods will also invite *positivity* and good fortune to your life. How? Let us understand this a little more in detail.

A few years into my practice, I began to be known as somebody who could treat chronic conditions when all else had failed. People who could not get their weight, sugar, cholesterol or cancer in control reached out to me. Families of cancer patients, on whom specialist doctors had given up, contacted me. And slowly, I started seeing the clinical difference between what nutrition experts were doing and what I was helping my patients do. I was doing three things:

1. Helping patients change the way they ate their food to release toxins.
2. Making them do their breath work differently to repair digestion.
3. Helping them change their response to stress with mind-body interventions.

If I had done only one or two out of the three, the clinical outcomes would not have been possible. Releasing of toxins is not just a physical process; it is also an emotional one. When we react to our environment and our loved ones and continue to simmer in toxic relationships without expressing our feelings, the emotional toxins can destroy us much more than the pizza you eat once a week.

Yes, you read that right.

Being under heavy stress shortens our life expectancy by 2.8 years.[1] Living healthy 80–90 per cent of the time and indulging in excesses 10 per cent of the time is absolutely fine as long as your response to stress is good. When you follow the programme listed in Part Two, you will reach a stage of reduced response to stress. Hence, physical release of toxins is related to reducing your emotional response to stress. Beautiful, isn't it? All you did was cleanse yourself and your mind started getting calmer.

So how do you understand that you are stressed out? A lot of people do not even acknowledge stress. Here is a simple test. Just look at the symptoms listed below and understand what applies to you:

1. Your skin fluctuates between getting acne to excess oiliness to pigmentation.
2. You have unexplained periods of hair fall.

3. You pick at your nails. It could be biting them or taking off the skin on the sides of the nail.
4. You have poor libido.
5. Your sleep pattern is disturbed.
6. You have recently experienced memory decline.
7. You experience unexplained headaches.
8. You suffer from acidity/bloating/constipation.

Many of these signs were discussed in Part One but, specifically, the above signs are directly connected to your stress levels. And we all know that stress is the biggest toxin we carry around on our conscience. It can affect our heart, our stomach, our energy levels and our lifespan. So, releasing stress as a toxin is an integral part of the shuddha programme.

The first thing I understood from my own illness and journey of recovery was that the body has to be imbalanced in some ways to allow the excess of something inside us that causes the disease. We are meant to repair and heal—that is the way nature has made us. There are some people who make minor changes and demonstrate drastic results and there are others who struggle all through their lives with poor results. The key element in these clinical differences is how we respond to stress. Only changing the way you eat is half the story and half the treatment. I focus on helping people change their response to stress so that the absorption of food and nutrients is higher, the digestive repair is better and, as a result, the toxin release is more efficient. And that is what I do differently in order to get clinically evidenced results for disease reversal.

It took me a lot of suffering to arrive at this result. This is my fourth book and I have talked about being a rheumatoid arthritis warrior in every book of mine. If you have not read my previous books, I will give you a quick recap. In 2006,

I was diagnosed with this autoimmune condition and as per medical science, autoimmune conditions are incurable. The patient is put on immunosuppressants, steroids and chemotherapy drugs in order to manage symptoms of the disease. In rheumatoid arthritis, specifically, the immune system attacks the joints—first the small joints and then the large joints. Younger people are more prone to it if they have poor immunity, high emotional sensitivity and if they live in a high-stress environment. I had all this. I was in a leadership position in a large Fortune 500 multinational company, earning well, globetrotting; I had a happy marriage and a beautiful child. But I still contracted this condition because my response to stress was poor. Everything I have written in this book has been tried by me on myself before it was implemented on my patient base across the world. And that is why I am so confident in the way forward for you. If someone healthy, balanced and in a happy relationship could attract an incurable condition, then anyone can. I had excess pain, joint deformities and my poor response to stress made my digestive system weaker. Under those circumstances, toxin release is poor, resulting in increasing inflammation levels.

Every single day that you wake up feeling the need to sleep, tired after eight hours of sleep, you are carrying the stress that is keeping you away from a healthy lifestyle. Follow the steps in the next chapter to release the stress and welcome a high energy life!

Chapter 2

Toxins and Well-Being

Now that you have understood that response to stress is a key factor in releasing toxins, we are going to dive deep into how to release this; you have to also understand the connection between toxins and well-being. I will give you an example which you can relate to very well: every time we are stressed out, we are in a poor mood. There are two ways that people react when they are stressed out and in a poor mood:

1. **They lash out at other people.** This means people around you, who may have nothing to do with the stress you are carrying, are bearing the brunt of your stress. These could be your loved ones and they will put up with your stress levels and erratic moods for a while before they begin to start reacting themselves. So instead of being the person who holds a loving family together, you begin to become the person who people want to avoid because they don't know when you will erupt. This is not your fault; it is just the level of stress you are carrying and not acknowledging. You can blame your work, sleep deprivation, lack of exercise or poor eating habits. Whatever your reasons are, they are detrimental to your own well-being. Other people will end up forgetting this momentary anger from you and move on, but the damage you create inside yourself in holding on to the most severe toxin known

to humankind—stress—can be quite ravaging for your health, especially your heart health.

2. **They hold a grudge.** Some people do not react with erratic moods or outbursts. They end up keeping quiet; holding a grudge. Holding onto a grudge can significantly impact your mental and physical health. 'When we hold onto grudges and resentment, it's like drinking poison and expecting the other person to get sick,' says Angela Buttimer, a licenced psychotherapist at Thomas F. Chapman Family Cancer Wellness at Piedmont.[2]

People who hold a grudge are at a higher risk for chronic pain and kidney issues as toxins are not released properly due to an overwrought digestive system. It is perfectly normal for many people to be in overlapping categories. However, being short-tempered when you are upset or stressed out and holding grudges against people who have wronged you for something will cause you more suffering than them. Holding on to stress suppresses our immune system and blocks the release of toxins.

So where does this stress come from? When you hold a grudge, you are reliving the events that happened which caused the grudge in the first place. Your brain does not know what is real and what is imagined. If you replay the same incident that upset you in your brain—and that incident may have occurred three months or one year ago—the brain reacts like it is happening right now. Since it is the brain that sends the agitation and stress signal to the rest of the body, the excess cortisol begins even with the memory of something that upset you. The feeling of being a victim or somebody who has been wronged suppresses immunity. This leads to chronic stress which raises our inflammation levels and cortisol levels, both of which will invite disease. And when grudges, toxins, hormones and/or inflammation are in excess in the human body, they all become the toxins that erode well-being.

On the other hand, letting go and forgiveness connect to the parasympathetic nervous system and release feel-good hormones like oxytocin, thereby reducing stress levels and cortisol levels. It is difficult to let go of a grudge or forgive somebody. But we don't do it for them, we do it for ourselves. We forgive so that *we* can release the stress and toxins and move on to a better quality of life.

Forgiveness and letting go are part of the detoxification process. Without letting go of grudges, it is impossible for you to have a cleansed mind and body. Yes, of course, it is difficult to do, that is why below are a few tried-and-tested techniques on how to forgive and let go for your own well-being.

Step One: Permit Yourself to Feel the Pain

Research in integrative medicine shows that avoiding negative emotions is detrimental to the immune system. Acknowledge and accept the fact that you have a grudge. If you do not even recognize that there is hurt and resentment inside, cleansing it and moving on becomes difficult. Find a safe territory to talk about this grudge. It could be a neutral friend or a counsellor. If you don't have either option, write it in a journal or record it on your phone. When we write about it or talk about it, even if it is to a recorder in our phone, we are beginning to come to terms with the fact that someone we least expected to wrong us, has hurt us. It happens to everybody and acknowledging and accepting it is the first step towards starting your cleansing process.

Step Two: Revisit Your Feelings

Once you have talked about or written about the grudge, give it one week and then revisit your feelings. If you have written it in the journal or recorded your voice, read it or play it back to yourself. Do you associate with those feelings as strongly? Ask yourself if you can change the situation or the person. If the situation or the person's behaviour is not in your control, free yourself of the responsibility of somebody else's behaviour. The moment you step out and look at this entire scenario as a third person, you will realize that the hurt you are carrying is not worth it. It's highly likely that the person who hurt you isn't even aware that they did.

Step Three: Establish Boundaries

If you are not ready to forgive someone, it is best to distance yourself physically and emotionally from them. Time will help you have a more peaceful response to their existence. It could be a loved one, a work colleague or a relative. Sometimes our frequencies do not match and this causes emotional turbulence and toxicity. If you cannot physically distance yourself from the person, make sure you have an emotional distance. Respond less to text messages, emails and conversations. For a while, reduce communication or stop it completely. The other person or people may find it strange, but when you are consistent in your behaviour, they will learn to accept it. They may even start respecting your boundaries or treating you with more care.

Step Four: Stop Being Available to People Who Take You for Granted

Sometimes, out of sheer love, we make ourselves available to people unconditionally. Unfortunately, not everybody values this. This starts a cycle of them taking us for granted and us lowering our own self-worth. Lack of confidence and lack of self-worth suppress the immune system and become heavy to carry if you are looking at a free and cleansed mind and body. For such people, it is imperative that you distance yourself and not be available at their beck and call. It could be a spouse, a child or a boss. Like I said in the previous step, establish your boundaries more particularly and firmly with these people. Especially for parents, this becomes important because parents, especially mothers, are unable to let go and wean off their children to allow them to be independent. Look at it this way: if you help your child cope better and become independent, the child will be able to look after themselves better in the real world when you are not around. By distancing yourself from them, you are enabling and empowering them to lead their own lives with confidence. Don't be available all the time to feed them, clean their room and help with homework after a certain age. By the time children are in their mid-teens, the parent has to let them go and give them space. On the other hand, if it is a spouse or a boss, do only the absolutely necessary tasks. As time goes by, they will get the message that you are no longer accessible as per their whims and convenience. This will help you set your emotional boundaries and protect yourself from getting hurt.

Step Five: Understand That Being Unforgiving Increases Your Pain

Once you have started following the earlier steps, you have already taken the first step towards living mindfully. You are watching your own behaviour and correcting your behaviour by not being available to people who take you for granted or who hurt you. By doing this, you are putting yourself first. This is an extremely important step in the mindfulness practice. When we become mindful of how we live and of our behaviour, we protect ourselves from piling up negative emotions about the people around us. When we do that, people around us lose the power to hurt us. And this brings us freedom. Of course, true forgiveness will take time; it is not an overnight process. But when you take the first step, with every single new day, you are letting go of some hurt, anger and resentment.

Step Six: Forgive Yourself

In the entire process of creating boundaries, we start feeling guilty. Some of us also go through the process of feeling that we invited the behaviour of the other person. This could not be further from the truth. Just remember, unknowingly, you also may have hurt somebody and that is exactly what happened to you. So do not hold yourself responsible for someone else's behaviour or misbehaviour. Be kind to yourself, forgive yourself and start practising the next step of regaining your self-confidence and self-respect. When you do that, you empower yourself to become strong and let go of the past. Forgiveness is a gift you give to yourself.

Step Seven: Visualize Forgiveness

Visualization is an extremely powerful technique that can help you let go of grudges. This is part of the self-affirmation techniques I have used successfully for people with chronic pain and emotional conflicts. The detoxification process for such people becomes much more difficult due to holding onto grudges. Self-affirmation has demonstrated powerful effects—research suggests that it can minimize anxiety, stress and defensiveness associated with threats to our sense of self-worth.[3] Self-affirmations can remap the brain, increase self-worth, reduce response to stress and negativity and have clinically-evidenced neurological benefits for people who are prone to anxiety and have blocked the process of emotionally cleansing themselves from those who have hurt them. Self-affirmations, in short, help you let go of feeling like a victim and empower you to become self-confident and believe in your own self-worth. Here is how you can visualize it:

Prepare for It

Sit in a comfortable position, either on a chair, sofa or bed. Your back should be completely supported but you should not be slouching. Put a stopwatch on for 60 seconds and close your eyes. Inhale deeply, exhale deeply and repeat. Continue the process till your stopwatch stops. In just 60 seconds, you will feel the difference. Your mind is now calm.

Visualize the person. When we carry hurt, it is usually from someone we love or someone important to us. After your breath is calm, with your eyes closed, visualize this person sitting in front of you. And repeat these words slowly:

I forgive you.
I take away the power from you to hurt me.
I love myself.
I embrace myself as I am.
Your hurt taught me a lesson and it is time for me to let go of that hurt.
I am letting you go and I am moving on.
I am worthy of happiness.
I am happy.
I emit positive energy.
I invite positive energy.
I have no space for negativity.

While you say this, visualize this person disappearing. Now, open your eyes slowly.

Repeat the above self-affirmation exercise every day for 10 days to let go of hurt and grudges. You can put on some soothing instrumental music while you do it. Make sure you are in a quiet room by yourself and you verbalize all this loudly instead of saying it only in your mind. This cleansing is going to help you let go of stress and anxiety and pent-up emotions which are the toxins blocking nutrient absorption. Once you have let go of your emotional toxins, the detoxification process in combination with the nutrition listed in Part Two, will be complete.

Many people mistake forgiveness for forgiving bad behaviour, but really, forgiveness and setting boundaries is the path to emotional freedom even for abusive behaviour you can't change. If you have an abusive loved one, you are no longer feeling repressed emotionally to what he or she did to hurt you. You become free.

Chapter 3

Emotional Shuddhi

A person who has mastered the art of letting go starts on a path of physical and emotional balance. And in this balance, there is no space for toxins to stay inside. We are all complete and holistic beings. When you follow the nutrition plan specified in Part Two and cleanse yourself emotionally with the steps I have given in the previous chapter, you will finally start to feel lighter, freer and healthier. Your energy will be better and your aura will be positive. The same people who may not have treated you with respect, start looking at you with new eyes. Your own self-worth demonstrates a behaviour to them that they need to respect. Ironically, if we do not respect ourselves, others will not either. It is not easy to be confident or have self-worth without following the steps of self-nurturing as written in the previous chapter. Self-love and self-nurturing are giant pillars for healing ourselves emotionally and allowing emotional toxins to be released.

Once your emotional toxins are released and your mind is calm, you are ready for true emotional shuddhi. This can be inculcated easily by integrating the habits below and making your digestive and immune system so strong that there is no space for toxins. Please remember, all these things work in combination with each other. You are not just mind, you are not just body, you are not just emotions, you are not just heart. You are all these and more, and that is why you have to step back and look at yourself as a holistic human being with a mind, body and soul that needs to be aligned. The simple steps written for physical and emotional nutrition will help you get in touch with your inner self, which is the subtle body, rather than the physical self, which is the gross body. This subtle body is more in touch with the self and does not allow emotional or physical toxins to enter. There is pride, which is different from ego, which helps you nurture yourself and create physical and emotional boundaries to block toxins.

Spend 20 minutes in a natural environment. This could be a window with a view, a bench in a park, the view of the sky from your terrace or the waves of the sea beckoning you from a beach. Whichever of these you have access to, is good enough. Sometimes it could just be a soft sofa in a quiet room where you are not disturbed. It doesn't matter. This is your natural environment where you feel most comfortable. Where do you take out the 20 minutes from? This is a question you have to ask yourself because prioritizing just 20 minutes in a day is much easier than piling up toxins and increasing your risk of diseases. This is an extremely effective way of releasing stress and repairing your digestive system to work more efficiently. It's also free! A study published in *Frontiers in Psychology*[4] revealed that just a 20-minute natural experience was enough to significantly reduce levels of cortisol, our stress hormone. But if people increased this time from 20 to 30 minutes of sitting or walking, cortisol levels dropped rapidly.

Practise the one-minute conscious breathing. Practise this simple one minute breathing technique throughout the day. Sit comfortably in a chair or sofa or lie down. Close your eyes and breathe deeply. Exhale. Repeat gently. Do this for just one minute. Do this at 11.00 a.m., 5 a.m. and 9.00 p.m.

You will feel the difference—it will change your response to stress. This one minute of conscious breathing needs to be part of your purified life.

We all breathe but we take this breathing process for granted. Becoming conscious of our breath is the start of mindful living. There are some of us who go from one task to the other and do not focus on our breath and that is known as shallow breathing. Shallow breathing increases our stress levels. On the other hand, there are some people—mostly senior business leaders with amazing ideas and execution capabilities—who get into conscious breathing. Also known as diaphragmatic breathing, this reduces our rhythm of breath and is directly associated with reduced levels of stress and increased levels of well-being. It stimulates our parasympathetic nervous system (PNS) which is responsible for our well-being.

The PNS is one of three divisions of the autonomic nervous system (ANS).[5] The PNS, often known as the 'rest and digest' system, conserves energy as it slows the heart rate, increases intestinal and gland activity, and relaxes the sphincter muscles in the entire gastrointestinal tract. Sphincters are specialized muscles located at the upper oesophagus (upper oesophageal sphincter, gastroesophageal junction, antroduodenal junction, ileocecal junction and the anus).

You don't need to check in to a yoga centre or sign up with a yoga teacher to learn conscious breathing. You can do this as a break when you are furiously working on the laptop and need to take a breather or after finishing cooking a meal when you need to sit under the fan. The one-minute breathing should be repeated a minimum of three times a day. Use your phone stopwatch, set it to 60 seconds, close your eyes and start breathing deeply. Just like we have intermittent fasting (which you are doing on a daily basis with my programme by finishing your dinner by 7.00 p.m. and having a 15-hour break till your first meal the next day), intermittent breathing helps us repair our digestive system and releases toxins. It also calms our response to stress and increases the happiness quotient.

This mindful or conscious breathing is over and above the breathing exercises given in Part Two. In the entire 24 hours, you are closing your eyes and are mindful about your breathing, even for three minutes, it will change your perspective towards your own health. And that is the turning point for all toxins to get released and your physical and emotional shuddhi to get balanced. The physical nutrition will connect with the emotional nutrition and help heal your gut and release the toxins. This is the holistic balance.

PART FOUR

The Holistic Detox Path

Whatever purifies you becomes the right path.

Chapter 1

Physical and Emotional Detox

The shuddha programme has helped you inculcate mindfulness in your food and eating habits. Now that you have understood the connection between toxins, stress, holding a grudge and the PNS, understanding how these are interlinked will be much easier. So if we take the steps from the entire book and recap them, what are we truly trying to achieve?

Let us look at the detox plan from an overview perspective. Here are the three pillars:

The Physical Detox

Following a daily rhythm of physical activities in a structured manner is extremely important for our body to heal. The steps written in Part Two, right from waking up on time to the morning exercises and breathing techniques to eating the foods as per the plan are important for the body's rhythm to stabilize. Timings, combinations and quantities all contribute towards this detox process. The healing is sequential—this means that in the stepladder of healing, you cannot go from step one to four as that would compromise the process of the detox. When you follow the four Rs, only then do the toxins get released properly. Once there is continuous nourishment and release of toxins due to this *uninterrupted* input, the body begins to respond to a higher living. The structure and rhythm is necessary to send a message to your body that the toxins have no place in it now.

The Emotional Detox

The breathing exercises given in Part Two, the emotional cleansing with the self-affirmation exercise and the conscious breathing throughout the day as per Part Three are all part of the emotional detox. The *let it go* exercises release excessive stomach acids which are formed when our anxiety levels are high. When we start releasing the causes of our stress, like holding in bitterness, poor self-confidence, low self-esteem and body image, the symptoms also start disappearing. The symptoms of emotional toxins have already been discussed, so when we apply these techniques for our emotional detox, we are going directly to the source and eliminating the causes from their origin. It is only then that we are emotionally shuddha.

Following the Mindful Combination

When we combine the physical and emotional nutrition, we detox and heal. The self-affirmations and one-minute breathing exercises throughout the day help us stay calm in the face of stress all around us. The same things that bothered us earlier begin to seem less significant. We start to become more tolerant of other people and situations because our self-defence towards allowing negativity around us to enter us is higher. When this physical and emotional detox combination is followed mindfully, the human body and mind repair. Repair work cannot happen before the release of toxins, letting go of negative emotions or forgiveness. Once you forgive, let go and move on, only then can you experience santosh, the highest form of living. When we have this state of mind, we accept what we cannot change, strive towards what we can and count our blessings for what we have. This form of higher living in Ayurveda invites gratitude and positivity. And you tell me, who does not want to invite positivity into their lives?

To invite positivity, we have to let go of the past to make place for a bright and healthy future.

So in practical terms, how are these three pillars implemented? Here I would like to share some patient case studies with you.

Chapter 2

Attitude Is Everything

Manya and Ranjita[1] are sisters married to two brothers and live in Hyderabad. They live in a joint family and are just two years apart. Their genetic make-up, naturally, is similar. They both came to me with severe joint pains, bloating, occasional constipation, forgetfulness and excess weight. Both were similar ages and dealing with very poor quality of life due to their symptoms. Aged 34 and 36, they both had a lot of hormonal fluctuations, acne, coarse hair and mood swings. They woke up feeling tired and did not look forward to their daily routines, tasks at work or doing anything for their loved ones or even spending happy times with their family. Both also had borderline hypothyroidism, PCOS and high erythrocyte sedimentation rate (ESR), a non-specific inflammation marker.

ESR[2] is an inflammation marker which is marginally high in the presence of an infection or with hormonal distress, which both of them had. However, their ESR levels were above 50 which is alarming. Normally, without the presence of cough, cold, infections or a chronic disease, levels of ESR should not be this high. Even with an infection, ESR levels go up to 35 or 40. It is only in patients of severe chronic diseases that these levels are high but both Manya and Ranjita did not have a chronic condition like autoimmune diseases, cancer[3] or type two diabetes. What they had was chronic stress. Cortisol levels were high, and a mild fatty liver meant that the liver was not fully efficient in the detoxification process. This resulted in both of them being listless, with a poor libido. We discussed the causes of their stress (individually via counselling sessions) and since my detox programme does not focus only on the superficial detoxification process, their response to stress required reworking in order to help them heal.

So for them, my shuddha programme was perfect.

When I began their treatment, their despair was evident. Since they were sisters who had married into the same family, the emotional challenges they faced were similar in terms of expectations from the rest of the family, and their food had been fairly healthy for many years now. They were all vegetarian, and everybody had at least one vegetable and cut salad at lunch and dinner. Consumption of ghee, yoghurt and milk was high and they were very conscious of the fact that they procured this from an organic farm as they had growing kids who needed cow's milk for better growth and strong bones. Even though milk and milk products were not part of their plan as their body at this stage did not require them, I encouraged them to continue to give it to their children, as it is crucial for brain development and growth till the age of 18. I reassured both to take support from each other for recipes and do the breathing exercises and movement together so that one could encourage the other.

The combinations and steps were explained to both Manya and Ranjita over video sessions and emails. Complete charts were sent to them to follow step by step. It should have been an ideal way to heal—with a companion right at home. We feel so much more motivated this way, rather than doing it in isolation, right? However, as I continued to do my sessions and healing with them, putting them on a similar plan as listed in this book, the stark differences began to emerge.

Manya began healing rapidly. After four months of treatment with me, Manya's ESR and cortisol levels were back in range, her acne had disappeared and her joint pains were negligible. Her energy levels were high and she kept thanking me for this new lease of life she had got. She had always faced a problem of weight since childhood and because of this, her spouse had hesitated taking her out with him for friends' get-togethers. I had felt bad, I had asked her if she wanted to start couples counselling with a good counsellor, but she refused. She confessed that she first wanted to get her own health back via the detoxification process. When her husband saw her emerge as this beautiful young woman, he began to pay more attention to her and their relationship improved. She lost 13 kilograms in the process and now looked like a young college girl. She experienced higher energy and they would go for walks together.

'You have given me a new lease of life,' she told me one day.

'You have given yourself one,' I told her. Without her commitment to self, this would not have happened.

When she began feeling better, she also started paying attention to her outward appearance. She no longer fit into her old clothes; she got a new wardrobe, she also got a new haircut. This enhanced look made her feel more confident. Her inner being and outer being were in balance with each other and her commitment to continue to follow this path till date—it has been seven years—has been very strong.

Ranjita, on the other hand, would keep sending me emails on a daily basis about her pain levels not improving. She struggled with the chart, kept emailing me that she could not follow it completely because of some reason, ranging from not getting the time to not liking the food to not feeling like following it. She lost six kilograms in four months, her hair fall reduced only marginally and the acne, though reduced, kept coming back. Her ESR and cortisol levels reduced but did not come back in range.

So why did these two young and beautiful women struggling with their health issues heal so differently, despite having the same issues and being on the same detox plan with me?

Manya was a believer. Manya's optimism in following everything helped her stick to the structure and made her body adapt to the rhythm of the physical detox. From day one, Manya began the discipline with complete faith. She would just read and follow, without questioning anything. She had pain, she had negativity and pessimism, but she trusted the process. Slowly, she began to look for positive signs which started emerging because of her discipline of follow through. Because of the physical detox, she began to see signs of healing that motivated her to adapt to the emotional detox techniques more easily. In one of her conversations with me, she told me, 'I had tried everything, nothing worked. So I thought let me give this my 100 per cent.'

Ranjita doubted it would work. Just like Manya, Ranjita had also tried everything but her perspective was different. Her attitude was sceptical and she kept wondering if this would work. She had signed up because Manya had been excited about it and not because she believed that she could heal. She did not believe that changing what she eats and or modifying her habits would help her if doctors had not been able to. She always ate healthy, she told me. 'Your suggestions are the same as what I have already been eating,' she said one day, grudgingly. I agreed, but counselled her that the combinations, timings, quantities and the way it was cooked were all very different. I had also eliminated items that were causing her hormonal distress and had included emotional detox techniques that would repair her digestive system and liver. But she found the breath work boring. She would do it for 50 or 100 counts and abandon it. This lack of belief made her do all her tasks in a half-hearted manner. Her discipline was poor. The result was evident.

The human body and mind are stronger than we have been made to believe. The ability of our body to repair itself is much higher. Medical science has yet not captured how our mind works because it is not an organ. The strength of our mind pushes our body to heal. In Ayurveda, each cell is considered to be inherently an essential expression of pure intelligence hence called self-healing science. Just like we live in an intelligent universe comprising energy, each cell in our body also has its own intelligence. Giving it wings and positivity helps us heal our cells.

You could choose to be Manya or Ranjita. If we respect the intelligence of our mind and give it the positivity it needs, our paths will be full of the marvels of healing, as experienced by Manya and lakhs of other people who have healed themselves without the support of medical science.

PART FIVE

The Shuddha Life

Chase your dreams with your new cleansed life.

Chapter 1

11 Signs That You Have Been Detoxed

Once you have read through Part One to Four and implemented specifications to your life—a six-week process—you will begin to feel some fairly-sparkling effects of my shuddha programme. So what will these be?

You experience positive energy. When the mind-body balance is pure and the nutrients are getting absorbed efficiently, the biggest shift in our quality of life is higher and positive energy. When we emit this positivity, we also invite positivity. So many people on my shuddha programme start inviting happy events and positive people, who get attracted to them and want to form a work or personal relationship with them. This happens because when you are in a state of high positive energy, you are attracting and manifesting that the same energy come back to you.

1. **You will lose weight if you need to.** This is the most beautiful aspect of my detox plan. Apart from the couple of kilos that you will lose in the first four weeks, if you do not need to lose more weight, your weight will stabilize. However, if you need to lose more weight, the body and mind will strive for the perfect balance of releasing toxins and excess bad fat. And hence, you will continue to lose weight if you need to.

2. **Your reports will be better.** If you have truly followed all the three pillars of the detox in the combinations listed, now is a good time to get your blood tests done to see the wonderful changes. For those of you who had high sugar (HBA1C), cholesterol, triglyceride, fatty liver, inflammation markers like ESR and C-reactive protein, this would have started tumbling down towards being back in range. This is the clinical sign for you that your body is healing, and the toxins have finally disappeared, leaving behind a gut that absorbs nutrients and makes the immune system strong.
3. **Your kidneys will become stronger.** Reduced hypertension is usually a sign of good kidney function. Uncontrolled high blood pressure for a long period of time can cause arteries around the kidneys to narrow, weaken or harden. These damaged arteries are incapable of distributing enough blood to the kidney tissue. The damaged kidney arteries then stop filtering blood well, leading to kidney damage. After following my programme, take your blood pressure readings after waking up in the morning every day for five days. If you have high BP, and are on medication, this BP would have come down, demonstrating that you need to go to your doctor and get your dosages reduced. This has happened to all my patients who are on my shuddha programme, including people who are older—even my 82-year-old father was asked to stop his blood pressure medication after he began my programme!
4. **Your skin will become brighter.** There are various reasons for this. Your gut is now cleansed and you no longer have stuck toxins in your colon if you are excreting stool at least twice a day. Constipation is a big cause for

toxins. Secondly, this is a sign that the liver is performing efficiently. When the liver is sluggish, we get pigmentation or dark patches on various parts of our body, including our face. Poor oxygen levels in the body can lead to malfunctioning of the liver because oxygen is required for the release of dead red blood cells (RBCs), toxins and distribution of iron in the body. It was earlier believed that the spleen performs these functions of RBC removal and iron distribution but new research has shown that this is the job of our liver.[1] RBCs have an average lifespan of 120 days and need to be released by the liver out of the body once they die. Poor liver performance is linked to iron toxicity in the body. Iron distribution, again, cannot happen in the absence of oxygen. The liver performs much better, hence reducing fatty liver, increasing the release of toxins and making the skin brighter and healthier because the toxins from the skin have been released by the liver. The pranayamas and the breath work in your detox programme help reverse this process by increasing oxygen levels. The plants prescribed in Part One of this book help you stay oxygenated.

5. **You will have clearer skin.** Acne, pimples and pigmentation will all start disappearing now. With the detox programme, the oxygenation levels are good and the intake of good fat along with vegetables is in balance, leading to a cleansed digestive system and prevention of constipation. This automatically makes the skin, our largest organ, demonstrate the positive effects of the detoxification programme by glowing with cleansed energy.

6. **Your general mood improves.** People around you will start noticing this before you do. When the toxins are

released from our mind and body and we are no longer carrying any physical or emotional load, we feel freer. We feel calmer. This reduces our response to stress and increases our tolerance for the same tasks that used to irritate us earlier. So, whether you are at work or at home, people around you will start noticing that you are mostly in a good mood and suddenly, you will become popular again!

7. **Your brain functions more efficiently.** Your brain's freshness levels increase, energy levels become high and you realize that you can work much more efficiently. Whether it is organizing kitchen supplies, children's homework, guiding your community or friends or projects in your office, your brain will function at top speed. The earlier sluggishness which was caused by the toxins would have disappeared. This efficient functioning is because your sleep cycle has become streamlined to the rhythm of my detoxification programme. We are meant to sleep at a particular time and wake up at a particular time. When we stop working with our own body's rhythm and are up till late and then wake up late, the brain does not perform efficiently. Waking up every day at 7.00 a.m. and doing the exercises and breath work invigorates our brain and cleanses out the previous day's sluggishness. Sleep repairs and reduces brain fatigue, leading to a fresher and more competent brain.

8. **Your periods become regulated.** If you are a woman on this programme, by the third cycle, the discomfort before periods starts disappearing. Your cycles become more regular and mood swings before periods reduce or completely disappear. Many women also experience a shrinking of ovarian cysts and endometrial lining after

my detoxification programme. This is an added benefit, as in medical science, the only treatment available for these problems is surgical or via medications, which come with their own set of side effects and long-term impact on the quality of life.

9. **You become calmer.** Serotonin is responsible for your feelings of happiness.[2] Serotonin is a neurotransmitter that acts as the body's natural antidepressant and pain reliever. It also helps regulate your sleep cycle and other processes in your body, including your appetite. Once your detox is complete and you are living the shuddha life, your serotonin levels remain balanced. This naturally reduces your response to stress and makes you look at everything with calmness and reason. Your moods are better and they do not oscillate from one end to the other. This balance brings about better relationships. With this programme, you have adequate levels of serotonin, and you feel emotionally stable and calm. This ensures remarkably higher levels of energy and focus.

10. **Your gratitude is higher.** The release of toxins brings up oxytocin levels, our love hormone. Your stress hormone, cortisol, on the other hand, is lowered. When we decrease cortisol through the detoxification process, heart rate and blood pressure reduce, and the immune system is able to enhance its function in protecting us from viruses and bacterial infections. The feeling of love and gratitude combined with reduced heart rate and BP brings about a state of harmony. Your gratitude for your environment, your surroundings, your loved ones and for having this able and efficient body and mind becomes higher. This is because you have moved away from a life of running from one task to the other, towards mindful living.

When you have experienced this beautiful mindful living, you don't want to let it go. So in the next chapter, we will talk about how to continue the stability of your mind-body connect being in harmony with each other and allowing you to continue to live a higher quality of life.

Chapter 2

How To Live the Detox Life—Travel Tips

Remember your state of mind before this programme? There was stress, so now have the triggers for stress gone away? No. Instead, it is your response to stress that has changed. Your inner being has become balanced in the same old environment. Most of us look for escapes and different cities or different environments or better jobs to find that inner peace. When we start going in and connecting with what is best for ourselves to maintain the mind-body-soul connection, we realize that the happiness is within us. Now that you have found that happiness within and are living mindfully, you need to continue it to be able to experience high energy and better brain efficiency so that you can get noticed for your good work in the office, and a higher gratitude and self-love quotient. Your family is important to you and you are important to them. For their sake and for your own sake, you need to be in harmony with yourself to be able to nurture them.

Always remember: if you do not self-nurture and release your physical and emotional toxins, you will not be able to find the space to nurture others.

We all like to travel, be it for work or leisure. Travel is a pleasure that cleanses the brain, releases stress and helps us form new beautiful experiences. When we travel to unknown places, the learning experience combined with the beauty of the place helps us form neural pathways in the brain that increase our brain power, memory and enhance our mental well-being. So as part of your shuddha life, I would strongly recommend travel. Here are some tips:

1. **Drive instead of taking a flight or train.** Travel as an experience has become even more precious during the lockdown period. But travel does not necessarily have to be by air or train. One condition for travel is explore places around you and go on road trips. For a couple of years after the lockdown is over, it will still be safer to drive out to places in order to protect your immune system. Every Indian city or town has getaways around it. Take your map, Google the information and plan a fun holiday with the family. What driving out also does is it helps you manage your resources and food better. You can carry the basics of your life, for example, flaxseed or extra virgin olive oil, pouches of almonds and pistachios, apples and green tea. Most of these things are not available in smaller resorts or home stays. What is available is the relaxing experience, the scenic surroundings and the lack of hustle and bustle of your city or town life, which in itself will help you feel completely relaxed. At this time, when you have the basics of your new detox life, you will ensure that the experience of relaxation on a holiday with loved ones is even more enhanced.
2. **Request and consume your preferred food choices.** The local cuisine and new chefs are waiting for you when you are looking at exotic homestays or resorts. Get in touch with the chef or the owner of the homestay and tell them that you prefer more vegetables in your meals

(while keeping their local flavours and style of cooking intact) and would like a cut salad at every meal. You can combine these with all the appetizing local preparations that the homestay has prepared to pamper you and your loved ones. This way the balance on your plate will still be maintained and you will be able to enjoy different tastes and flavours.

3. **Customize just 20 per cent of your meal.** We don't want to be on any nutrition plan when we travel. But when we are living mindfully, we can enjoy 80 per cent of the foods on the holiday if we are careful about having the 20 per cent essentials to keep our mind and body shuddha. These are:
   1. Infuse your fresh cut salad with flaxseed oil or extra virgin olive oil.
   2. Consume green tea thrice a day—once on waking up, once mid-morning and once early evening.
   3. With the green tea, you can combine the antioxidant packed almonds and pistachios or any local fruits available at the homestay that are low in sugar. Remember: watermelon, cheeku, mangoes and grapes in larger quantities and bananas are all high sugar fruits, so these should be avoided. There is an array of local fruits of which a small bowl can be happily devoured in the scenic holiday environment, once a day.

4. **Indulge but don't overeat.** It is natural to want to pamper ourselves on a holiday by indulging in our favourite snacks and delicacies. There is no harm in indulging. However keep your quantities low so that the benefits of the detox programme are not completely lost. Remember: 20 per cent aakash on your plate and your stomach ensures that

there is space for digestive juices to absorb nutrients from food and release toxins. Eating 20 per cent less will almost always ensure that your toxin release is efficient all through your life even if you are not eating a balanced and healthy meal.

5. **If you like alcohol, stick to wine.** We often feel like rewarding ourselves on a holiday by indulging in a little drinking. However, hard liquor can increase inflammation levels whereas red wine—not port wine—will have the opposite effect if had in very small quantities. There are a lot of Indian wines available across the country and you could have just 120 millilitres a couple of times during your holiday to enjoy and indulge.

6. **Explore your surroundings.** Don't sit in the room or on your phone. Go out, even if there is nothing to see, your homestay or resort itself is beautiful. I am sure you chose it because of its greens, gardens, fresh air and the fact that it is away from the hustle and bustle of the city. Utilize the luxury of having the greenery around you—walk on grass every morning and evening. The pleasure of walking on grass also has health benefits: it is called 'earthing'. The minerals from the earth get absorbed through the soles of our feet and start releasing inflammation and stress. This is scientifically evidenced in many studies.[3] While doing this, you will also ensure that your circulation is efficient and physical activity is maintained.

7. **Don't forget your breath work.** In such amazingly clean surroundings and pure air, it would be criminal not to inhale the purity. Finish off with your pranayama in the morning and set aside time in the evening for some one-minute deep breathing sessions with your family. In fact, it can become a game! Make everybody sit, children

included, and play the breath game. The rules of the game are as follows: everyone will take five deep breaths only. The person who takes the maximum time and does it the slowest, yes, the *slowest* and not the fastest, and finishes last, is the winner. This means they are taking long and deep breaths. Make sure there is a reward for the winner. The reward could be something small and not materialistic. It could be a special dessert for an older person; if it is a child, it could be extra time to play outdoors. Doing this will help your entire family manage their response to stress and enjoy the holiday to the fullest. It will also ensure that your deep breathing habit does not get affected.

Chapter 3

How To Live the Detox Life—Eating out

Once the lockdown is over, you can start ordering in or eating out. It is healthy to order in or eat out at least once a week in order to break the monotonous cycle of eating home-cooked food. It also gives the person who manages the kitchen a respite from their daily responsibilities. Now that you are more mindful of your living, you will also be more considerate to family members and ensure that everyone in the house gets this much deserved weekly break. So how do you ensure the balance when you are eating out?

Below are some eating out tips:

Do it just once a week. Even the best restaurants will reuse frying oil. And we know that reused oil can be potentially cancerous. So ensure that your eating out is no more than once a week, as doing this frequently will mean that the bad oil is going to raise your inflammation and toxin levels in the body.

Do it at lunch. Whether you are ordering in or eating out, the body can detoxify the effects of outside food much faster if it happens at lunch. So even if you are feeling bloated after this meal, you can do some exercise or breath work to cleanse and have a light dinner to negate the effects of this. If you do it at dinner, your sleep will be disturbed and you will not wake up fresh the next morning, hence spoiling the next day.

Keep the salad. No matter what you eat, whether it is fried or heavy, having a portion of salad with olive oil or flaxseed oil is essential to balance your plate and digestive system. While you enjoy the fried food, the salad and olive oil combination will protect your digestive system from its side-effects.

Try to be mindful. When we order in or eat out, the natural tendency is to overeat. Again, remember akash? Enjoying your favourite foods, including biryani, fried bhajia/pakoras, puris, samosas or heavy curries will have an impact on your digestive tract. But when you keep quantities less and savour the taste rather than having larger bites, you will realize that it is the taste of the food not the quantity that gives you joy. So be mindful, take smaller bites and focus your attention on the flavours of the food on your tongue and enjoy that. Didn't you want to eat out because you wanted a different flavour? If yes, then just relish that flavour and the aromas and you will realize that you don't need the quantities you used to eat earlier. Eating tasty food is a combination of the fragrance of the food and the taste on your palate. This is called the gastronomic experience. Even a small amount will give you the same santosh.

Your pharmacy is in your kitchen
Your purity in your breath
Your balance is in your mind
Not waking up fresh
Is a sign

Your new life is waiting to be met
So just leave behind
Disease and regret

Welcome to the shuddha life.

References

CHAPTER ZERO

1. Methotrexate, formerly known as amethopterin, is a chemotherapy agent and immunosuppresant. It is used to treat cancer, autoimmune diseases, ectopic pregnancies and medical abortions.

PART ONE

1. 'Air Pollution Puts Children at Higher Risk of Disease in Adulthood', *ScienceDaily*, 22 February 2021, www.sciencedaily.com/releases/2021/02/210222124613.htm. Accessed on 11 November 2011.
2. 'Weight Cycling is Associated With a Higher Risk of Death', *Endocrine Society*, 29 November 2018, https://www.endocrine.org/news-and-advocacy/news-room/2018/weight-cycling-is-associated-with-a-higher-risk-of-death. Accessed on 11 November 2021.
3. 'Declining Male Fertility Linked to Water Pollution', *ScienceDaily*, 20 January 2009, https://www.sciencedaily.com/releases/2009/01/090118200636.htm. Accessed on 11 November 2021.
4. Golomb, Beatrice Alexandra. 'Diplomats' Mystery Illness and Pulsed Radiofrequency/Microwave Radiation', *Neural Computation*, Vol. 30, No. 11, November 2018. DOI: 10.1162/neco_a_011336. Accessed on 11 November 2021.
5. 'Environmental Pollutants Could Impact Cellular Signs of Aging', *ScienceDaily*, 1 May 2019, https://www.sciencedaily.com/

releases/2019/05/190501082004.htm. Accessed on 11 November 2021.
6. 'Link between Air Pollution and Coronavirus Mortality in Italy Could Be Possible', *ScienceDaily*, 6 April 2020, https://www.sciencedaily.com/releases/2020/04/200406100824.htm. Accessed on 11 November 2021.
7. 'Environmental Pollution Increases Risk of Liver Disease, Study Finds', *ScienceDaily*, 1 June 2009, https://www.sciencedaily.com/releases/2009/05/090529085103.htm. Accessed on 11 November 2021.
8. 'Fried Food Risks: Toxic Aldehydes Detected in Reheated Oil,' *ScienceDaily*, 22 February 2012, https://www.sciencedaily.com/releases/2012/02/120222093508.htm#:~:text=02%2F120222093508.htm-Researchers%20have%20been%20the%20first%20to%20discover%20the%20presence%20of,a%20suitable%20temperature%20for%20frying. Accessed on 11 November 2021.
9. 'How Saturated Fatty Acids Damage Cells: Observations of Saturated and Unsaturated Fatty Acid Behaviour Could Impact Public Health', *ScienceDaily*, 1 December 2017, https://www.sciencedaily.com/releases/2017/12/171201181545.htm. Accessed on 11 November 2021.
10. 'America's Most Widely Consumed Oil Causes Genetic Changes in the Brain', *ScienceDaily*, 17 January 2020, https://www.sciencedaily.com/releases/2020/0½00117080827.htm. Accessed on 11 November 2021.
11. Gardner, Amanda. 'Plastic Bottles Release Potentially Harmful Chemicals (Bisphenol A) After Contact With Hot Liquids', *abcNews*, 24 March 2008, https://abcnews.go.com/Health/Healthday/story?id=4510256&page=1. Accessed on 11 November 2021.
12. 'Women With Polycystic Ovary Syndrome Have Higher BPA Blood Levels, Study Finds', *ScienceDaily*, 25 June 2010, https://www.sciencedaily.com/releases/2010/06/100621143602.htm. Accessed on 11 November 2021.
13. 'Chemical Exposure in the Womb From Household Items May Contribute to Obesity', *ScienceDaily*, 30 August 2012, https://

www.sciencedaily.com/releases/2012/08/120830135327.htm. Accessed on 11 November 2021.

14. Kader, Hanady. 'Chemical in Plastics Linked to Genital Abnormalities in Baby Boys', Seattle Children's Hospital, 30 August 2016, https://pulse.seattlechildrens.org/study-links-chemical-in-plastics-to-genital-abnormalities-in-baby-boys/. Accessed on 11 November 2021.

15. Sison, Gerardo. 'Does Your Body Really Replace Itself Every 7 Years?' Discovery, 1 August 2019, https://www.discovery.com/science/Body-Really-Replace-Itself-Every-7-Years. Accessed on 11 November 2021.

16. 'Does the Sun Move around the Milky Way?' Star Child Team, NASA, February 2000, https://starchild.gsfc.nasa.gov/docs/StarChild/questions/question18.html#:~:text=Yes%2C%20the%20Sun%20%2D%20in%20fact,Way%20is%20a%20spiral%20galaxy. Accessed on 11 November 2011.

17. Guerrero-Preston, Rafael, et al. '16S Rrna Amplicon Sequencing Identifies Microbiota Associated With Oral Cancer, Human Papilloma Virus Infection and Surgical Treatment', *Oncotarget*, 2016. DOI: 10.18632/oncotarget.9710. Accessed on 11 November 2021.

18. Nandakumar, T. 'Chemical Contaminants in Household Spices', *The Hindu*, 10 June 2015, http://www.thehindu.com/todays-paper/chemical-contaminants-in-household-spices/article7300031.ece. Accessed on 11 November 2021.

19. Savvy Soumya Misra and Sopan Joshi. 'Tracking Decades-Long Endosulfan Tragedy in Kerala', *DownToEarth*, 13 January 2017, https://www.downtoearth.org.in/coverage/health/tracking-decades-long-endosulfan-tragedy-in-kerala-56788. Accessed on 11 November 2021.

20. 'Organic Tturmeric Has Toxic Arsenic', Consumer Voice, 29 October 2014, http://consumer-voice.blogspot.in/2014/10/organic-turmeric-has-toxic-arsenic.html. Accessed on 11 November 2021.

21. 'Environmental Toxins Impair Immune System Over Multiple Generations' *ScienceDaily*, 2 October 2019, https://www.sciencedaily.com/releases/2019/10/191002144257.htm. Accessed

on 11 November 2021.
22. Harris, Gardiner. 'F.D.A. Finds 12% of U.S. Spice Imports Contaminated', *The New York Times*, 30 October 2013, https://www.nytimes.com/2013/10/31/health/12-percent-of-us-spice-imports-contaminated-fda-finds.html. Accessed on 11 November 2021.
23. Hou, Dianzhi, et al. 'Mung Bean (*Vigna radiata* L.): Bioactive Polyphenols, Polysaccharides, Peptides, and Health Benefits', *Nutrients*, Vol. 11, No. 6, June 2019. DOI: 10.3390/nu11061238. Accessed on 11 November 2021.
24. 'Sesame and Rice Bran Oil Lowers Blood Pressure, Improves Cholesterol', *ScienceDaily*, 19 September 2012, https://www.sciencedaily.com/releases/2012/09/120919190151.htm#:~:text=Sesame%20and%20rice%20bran%20oil%20lowers%20blood%20pressure%2C%20improves%20cholesterol,-Date%3A%20September%2019&text=Summary%3A,levels%2C%20according%20to%20new%20research. Accessed on 11 November 2021.
25. Kalpesh B. Panara and Rabinarayan Acharya. 'Consequences of Excessive Use of *Amlarasa* (Sour Taste): A Case-Control Study', *Ayu*, Vol. 35, No. 2, April–June 2014. DOI: 10.4103/0974-8520.146204. Accessed on 11 November 2021.

PART TWO

1. Wilbert, Steven A. 'Spatial Ecology of the Human Tongue Dorsum Microbiome', *Cell Reports*, Vol. 30, No. 12, March 2020. DOI: 10.1016/j.celrep.2020.02.097. Accessed on 11 November 2021.
2. 'Feed Your Genes: How Our Genes Respond To the Foods We Eat', *ScienceDaily*, 20 September 2021, https://www.sciencedaily.com/releases/2011/09/110919073845.htm. Accessed on 11 November 2021.
3. Suryatapa Bhattacharya and River Davis. 'Yes, You Can Sleep on the Job. Just Please Use the Nap Room', *The Wall Street Journal*, 19 September 2019, https://www.wsj.com/articles/yes-you-can-sleep-on-the-job-just-please-use-the-nap-room-11568905638. Accessed on 11 November 2021.

4. Reinberg, Steven. 'Expecting an Afternoon Nap Can Reduce Blood Pressure', *Health Day News*, 7 March 2019, https://www.webmd.com/hypertension-high-blood-pressure/news/20190307/an-afternoon-nap-may-lower-your-blood-pressure. Accessed on 11 November 2019.
5. 'Understanding the Chemicals Controlling Your Mood', CBHS Health, 15 August 2021, https://www.cbhs.com.au/mind-and-body/blog/understanding-the-chemicals-controlling-your-mood. Accessed on 11 November 2021.

PART THREE

1. Härkänen, Tommi, et al. 'Estimating Expected Life-Years and Risk Factor Associations with Mortality in Finland: Cohort Study', *BMJ Open*, Vol 10. No. 3, March 2020, DOI: 10.1136/bmjopen-2019-033741. Accessed on 11 November 2021.
2. 'What Does Holding a Grudge Do to Your Health?' Piedmont Healthcare, https://www.piedmont.org/living-better/what-does-holding-a-grudge-do-to-your-health. Accessed on 11 November 2021.
3. L. Legault, T. Al-Khindi and M. Inzlicht. 'Preserving Integrity in the Face of Performance Threat: Self-Affirmation Enhances Neurophysiological Responsiveness to Errors', *Psychological Science*, Vol 23, No. 12, October 2012. DOI: 10.1177/0956797612448483. Accessed on 11 November 2021.
4. Hunter, MaryCarol R. 'Urban Nature Experiences Reduce Stress in the Context of Daily Life Based on Salivary Biomarkers', *Frontiers in Psychology*, 2019, https://doi.org/10.3389/fpsyg.2019.00722. Accessed on 11 November 2021.
5. Science Direct, https://www.sciencedirect.com/topics/neuroscience/parasympathetic-nervous-system. Accessed on 11 November 2021.

PART FOUR

1. Names have been changed to protect privacy.
2. An erythrocyte sedimentation rate (ESR) is a type of blood test

that measures how quickly erythrocytes (red blood cells) settle at the bottom of a test tube that contains a blood sample. Normally, red blood cells settle relatively slowly. A faster-than-normal rate may indicate inflammation in the body. Inflammation is part of your immune response system. It can be a reaction to an infection or injury. Inflammation may also be a sign of a chronic disease, an immune disorder or some other medical condition; Medicine Plus, https://medlineplus.gov/lab-tests/erythrocyte-sedimentation-rate-esr/. Accessed on 11 November 2021.
3. I had ruled out cancer by getting their cancer markers checked and getting their uterus and ovaries scanned, and advised them to share these reports with their respective gynaecologists for confirmed medical advice.

PART FIVE

1. 'How the Body Disposes of Red Blood Cells, Recycles Iron: Accumulation and Removal of Aged or Damaged Cells Found to Take Place Mostly in the Liver, Rather than the Spleen', *ScienceDaily*, 18 July 2016, https://www.sciencedaily.com/releases/2016/07/160718132646.htm. Accessed on 11 November 2021.
2. Understanding the Chemicals Controlling Your Mood', CBHS Health, 15 August 2021, https://www.cbhs.com.au/mind-and-body/blog/understanding-the-chemicals-controlling-your-mood. Accessed on 11 November 2021.
3. Oschman, James L. 'The Effects of Grounding (Earthing) on Inflammation, the Immune Response, Wound Healing, and Prevention and Treatment of Chronic Inflammatory and Autoimmune Diseases', *Journal of Inflammation Research*, March 2015. DOI: 10.2147/JIR.S69656. Accessed on 11 November 2021.